THE GAUNTLET
A CHALLENGE TO THE MYTH OF PROGRESS

To Mr. Brad Payson, with thanks.

The Gauntlet

A Challenge
to the
Myth of Progress

A First Anthology
of the works of
Arthur J. Penty

Norfolk, VA
2003

The Gauntlet.

Old Worlds for New: a Study of the Post-Industrial State, Post-Industrialism, and *Towards a Christian Sociology* were first published by George Allen & Unwin, Ltd., of London, in 1917, 1922, and 1923, respectively. *Means and Ends* was published by Faber & Faber, Ltd., of London, in 1932. *Arthur J. Penty: His Contribution to Social Thought* was published by The Catholic University of America Press, of Washington, D.C., in 1941.

The selection from *Means and Ends* is copyright Faber & Faber, Ltd. The selection from *Arthur J. Penty* is copyright The Catholic University of America Press.

Preface, footnotes, typesetting, layout, and cover design copyright 2003 IHS Press.

IHS Press was unable to locate the holders of the original copyright to *Towards a Christian Sociology*. Any information leading to their identification would, therefore, be much appreciated. Additionally, the Editors wish gratefully to acknowledge assistance received from the Brynmor Jones Library, University of Hull, in locating a picture of Arthur Penty.

Notes to the original texts are included as footnotes. Editor's notes have been included as endnotes and are therefore to be found at the back of this edition.

ISBN: 0-9714894-9-1

Library of Congress Cataloging-in-Publication Data

Penty, Arthur J. (Arthur Joseph), 1875-1937.
  The gauntlet : a challenge to the myth of progress / by Arthur J. Penty.
        p. cm.
"A first anthology".
  ISBN 0-9714894-9-1 (alk. paper)
  1. Progress. 2. Social problems. 3. Capitalism--Religious aspects--Christianity. 4. Guilds--Europe--History. 5. Small business--Europe--History. I. Title.
  HM891.P46 2004
  303.44--dc21

                                                                2002155845

Printed in the United States of America.

Table of Contents

PAGE

INTRODUCTION..7
   by Dr. Peter Chojnowski

THE GAUNTLET

ARTHUR PENTY: HIS LIFE AND EARLY INFLUENCES.........15
   Arthur J. Penty: His Contribution to Social Thought

CURRENCY AND THE GUILDS..26
   Towards a Christian Sociology

MEANS AND ENDS..32
   Means and Ends

REGULATIVE AND PRODUCING GUILDS...............................54
   Towards a Christian Sociology

THE ETHICS OF CONSUMPTION...62
   Old Worlds for New: a Study of the Post-Industrial State

THE RETURN TO THE PAST..66
   Post-Industrialism

THE CHURCH AND THE COMMON MIND...........................80
   Towards a Christian Sociology

"*Modernism is bankrupt spiritually, morally, intellectually and politically, and because of this a reaction towards Tradition can only be a matter of time. Meanwhile the only reason why Modernists remain in the saddle is because Traditionalists have for so long been on the defensive that they have lost the habit of attack. They do not realize the strength of their position.*"

—Arthur J. Penty
Communism and the Alternative

INTRODUCTION

> One of the consequences of giving to spiritual values the foremost
> place is that we inevitably put the past before the present, because
> the great traditions of culture come from the past. Hence it has been
> that all great movements of human origin in history – good and bad
> – have had their beginning in a study of the past.
>
> —Arthur J. Penty
> "The Return to the Past"

D URING THE 19ᵀᴴ AND EARLY 20ᵀᴴ CENTURIES, there was
a group of scholars, theologians, philosophers, social critics, and poets who predicted the inevitable demise of the
capitalist economic system which was just developing in Continental
Europe, but which had been operative for 100 years in England.
Reading their works – here we include those of Arthur Penty,
Hilaire Belloc, and G.K. Chesterton – one is struck by the fact that
their analyses are more valid today than they were 70 or 80 years ago,
their predictions more likely to be imminently fulfilled. What they
predicted was nothing less than the collapse of the capitalist system.
In the case of Belloc, in his book *The Servile State,* it was predicted
that Capitalism would soon transform itself into an economic and
social system, which resembled the slave economies of pre-Christian
and early Christian eras.

Why did they predict such a collapse or inevitable transformation? In their writings many reasons are given, however, we can
narrow them down to three. The first they referred to as the "capitalist paradox." The paradox is a consequence of Capitalism being an
economic system that, in the long run, "prevents people from obtaining the wealth produced and prevents the owner of the wealth from

finding a market."[1] Since the capitalist strives both for ever greater levels of production and for lower wages, eventually "the laborer who actually produces, say, boots cannot afford to buy a sufficient amount of the boots which he himself has made."[2] This leads to the "absurd position of men making more goods than they need, and yet having less of those goods available for themselves than they need."[3]

The second reason is now more pertinent than when it was first given. The capitalist system, by its very nature, places the preponderance of wealth in the hands of a small minority. This monopoly on the money supply by banking and financial concerns becomes more absolute as the capital-needing consumer must go to the banks to borrow money. Usury, now called "interest," insures that those who first possess the money for loan will end up with a greater portion of the money supply than they possessed before the loan was issued. As wages stagnate and interest payments become increasingly impossible to make, a massive number of defaults will inevitably produce a crisis for the entire financial system.[4] When entire nations default on loans, there will be a crisis throughout the international system. Demise is, therefore, built into the very structure of the capitalistic system in which capital (i.e., all kinds of wealth whatsoever which man uses with the object of producing further wealth, and without which the further wealth could not be produced. It is a reserve without which the process of production is impossible[5]) is primarily in the hands of the few. As G.K. Chesterton rightly stated, the problem with Capitalism is that it produces too few capitalists!

The third fact concerning Capitalism which the Distributists, including Penty, thought would inevitably bring down the system or lead to its fundamental transformation was the *general instability* and *personal insecurity* which marks a full-blown capitalist economy. What accounts for this general feeling of insecurity and instability, which characterizes both the individual "wage-earner" and the society living under Capitalism, is the always-present fear of unemployment

---

[1] Hilaire Belloc, *Economics for Helen* (Hampshire, England: St. George Educational Trust, n.d.), p. 62.

[2] *Ibid.*   [3] *Ibid.*

[4] Cf. Hilaire Belloc, *Usury* (Hampshire, England: St. George Educational Trust, n.d.).

[5] Belloc, *Economics for Helen*, p. 13.

and, hence, of destitution, and the fact that a laborer's real wages leave him only enough money to cover the expenses of the day. Saving, so as to provide an economic hedge against the misfortune of unemployment or personal crisis, becomes almost impossible. This is a point that Arthur Penty emphasized in his book *Guilds, Trade, and Agriculture*, recently republished under the title *The Guild Alternative*.[6]

We have presented in this new Penty Anthology articles which both catalogue the long development of the credit-dependent, monopoly-driven, Liberal economic system and those which present a new vision of a human society and economy, which can stand as a substitute for the current system which steals man's labor from him, along with increasingly stealing his security and peace of soul. It is towards the end of this text where we find Penty making some of his most brilliant points. Here we find that he takes as a given what the "prudent" and the "practical" fail to see, *all* true and deeply grounded ideological presentations of a potential future of mankind, which would be distinctly better than the time period in which man currently finds himself, look to the past in order to find their models and ideals. It is towards the imitation of these models, already proven historically as being in accord with human nature and desire, that the philosopher directs the efforts of all those who will listen to his voice. It is well known that the re-establishment of the Guild system was the centerpiece of Arthur Penty's Distributist vision of a reformation of human economy and society. Throughout the articles of this anthology, Penty attempts to justify this intellectual retrieval of an institution that has been dead on the European scene since the French Revolutionary Chapelier Law of 1791. For us, who have endured the dismissive attitude of those who want to "work within the system," Penty's historical example of the profound consequences which followed in the wake of Sir Walter Scott's attempt at an imaginative reconstruction of the Medieval world – its ideals, loves, and longings – is truly heartening. Seeing the encroaching commercialization and cultural displacement of his own day, the period following the failure of the Stuart uprisings and the destruction of the power of the Highland chiefs, Scott attempted to preserve, at least in prose and verse, some memory of

---

[6] Cf. Arthur Penty, *The Guild Alternative* (Hampshire, England: St. George Educational Trust, n.d.), p. vi.

a life which was disappearing around him. As Cardinal Newman states in his *Apologia,* "the general need of something deeper and more attractive than what had offered itself elsewhere may be considered to have lead to his popularity; their mental thirst, feeding their hopes, setting before them visions which once seen, are not easily forgotten, and silently indoctrinating them with nobler ideas, which might afterwards be appealed to as first principles." This "mental thirst" of a people who had forgotten that the imagination is meant to *feed* and *fecundate* the intelligence was partially satisfied by the Oxford Movement in theology, the Pre-Raphaelite Movement in painting, and the Gothic Revival in architecture.

What enticed so many, during the course of the 19th century and beyond, to the historical Middle Ages is the obvious fact that there was possessed in this Age a "common mind" that made true fraternal society possible. Speaking of the ubiquitous Medieval desire to stamp out heresy, *mostly on the part of the State,* Penty contrasts this social understanding of the need for unity in *essential matters* (i.e., primarily religion) with Liberalism's corrosive and disengaging effects on the body politic. Liberalism's pervasive influence since the Napoleonic devastation of Europe has created a intellectual/religious situation where "for so long have men enjoyed freedom of thought and speech, for so long has such freedom been exalted as an end in itself, for so long has every false prophet who shakes the very foundation of right thinking and feeling enjoyed immunity that the average mind today is in such a hopeless state of confusion about everything that it is impossible to get agreement about any thing that really matters."

In the above, Penty has hit upon the Achilles' heel of the Liberal System. A social structure that is held together by an amorphous conglomeration of conflicting beliefs needs but the shock of reality to expose its intrinsic weakness. Society must be based upon discovered and accepted truth. Liberalism's first principles will allow neither for the attainment nor universal civic acceptance and enforcement of truth. Such an attainment and enforcement would mean the *end of the Liberal System.* That such an "end" might, also, be the occasion for a more perfect possession of human happiness seems to dawn on very few contemporary minds.

Of course, what Penty is most known for, and the topic which dominates this anthology, is the economic/social, dare we say "ideological," system that came to take the name of Distributism. Penty, we can truthfully say, became the ideologist of the Distributist League. This is statement is validated by the fact that his *Distributist Manifesto* was published by the Distributist League without alteration as Penty himself had written it shortly before his own death. This critique and attack on Liberal Capitalism, and the world which that system had created, was meant as an alternative to the "private-property-denying" ideologies of the other enemies of Capitalism, the Socialists and Communists. According to the *Manifesto*, "Distributism arose in opposition to the socialist and communist proposal to abolish the private ownership of property because, in the opinion of Distributists, without private property there can be no economic freedom, initiative or sense of personal responsibility. When property is nationalized the individual finds himself at the mercy of the State, to the tyranny of which resistance is impossible." Rather than simply rejecting Socialism as an attack on the "economic rights of the free individual" (i.e., the rights of those with assets and wealth to acquire more assets and wealth), "Distributists affirm that the evils which socialists trace to private ownership of property do not flow from the institution as such, but from the maldistribution of property which has come about as a consequence of laws favoring large ownership at the expense of small, and the absence of laws to prevent the misuse of money and machinery. By manipulating money and machinery, a few become rich and the many are dispossessed."

After reading much about the intrinsic rationality of the Distributist Third Way, it may be surprising to find in Penty's *Manifesto* a very significant caveat. After insisting upon the need to re-establish, in all of his independence and self-sufficiency, the small farmer and the rural-based craftsman, Penty reveals the profound realism of his outlook by stating, "Distributists are concerned to revive agriculture and to re-establish a peasantry on the soil. But they recognize that it is no use trying to plant them there until prices are fixed at a just level; for, until that is done, *to urge men with small capital to settle on the land is to urge them to commit economic suicide.*"

With the above we hit upon a point that is the crux of his economic and social theory. Moreover, it is the primary justification that he gives for his desire to resuscitate the Guilds as the fundamental economic structures of any Distributist System. It is Penty's historical thesis, a thesis that is extremely evocative and enlightening, that *the primary purpose for the existence of the Guilds in the Catholic Middle Ages was to enforce a system of just and fixed prices.* This, according to Penty, was the *raison d'etre* of the Guild System, as that system was slowly constructed, with the support of the Church, from the 11th century until its legal murder in late 18th century. According to Penty, "If prices and wages are to be fixed throughout industry, it will be necessary to organize Guilds to maintain them, for it would be impossible by means of bureaucracy to fix the price of more than a few staple things."

Of course, to fix prices at a just price, decided upon by Church, State, and Guild, would be to obviate the need for "finance" and strike at the very heart of Capitalism, which advances because of the power of the Capitalist to undersell the small man. If the small man cannot be undersold, he would find himself with an increase in his own capital, which itself would put him in a position to acquire real property. In one fell swoop, Capitalism is vitiated and the average man gains financial stability and power. It is not at all surprising to see how this new economic liberty would be achieved precisely by the suppression of the Capitalists' "right" to set prices according to "market forces." In the fixing of prices at a just rate, you would have the entrance of moral considerations into the economic calculus. We would actually have to ponder the "unthinkable" when treating economic concerns: "What does justice demand?" With this consideration, the human – and hence the philosophical and, ultimately, the theological – would necessarily have to be considered. Prices, rents, wages, a just human standard of living, and the intrinsic value of the work of a man would be considered, rather than just questions of "profitability." Indeed, how much longer in the course of human history must justice, family livelihood, the stability and peace of the familial generations, and fulfilling human work be sacrificed on the altar of profitability?

When we compare our own days to the days in which Arthur Penty was writing, we can immediately draw one serious point of contrast. The concentration of wealth and capital, the inadequacy of a man's pay to provide the basics of life and to provide for savings for the future, the lack of real property generously and broadly distributed – phenomena which Penty was all too aware of – is masked by the reality of easy credit. Easy credit, which ultimately is not "easy" at all on the borrower, anesthetizes the populace to the grim facts of capitalist monopoly. Since we seem to be able to get all the things that we want, the reality of real money being increasingly unavailable to the average man is lost in the delusionary state of the consumerist utopia. Only when the "benefit" of usurious credit is cut off do we realize that full extent of the problem.

The greatest problem with liberal Capitalism, however, is not the concentration of wealth or real property; the greatest "existential" problem created by Capitalism is the problem of the very meaning and reality of work. To work is essential to what it means to be a human being. Next to the family, it is work and the relationships established by work that are the true foundations of society. In modern Capitalism, however, it is productivity and profit which are the basic aims, not the providing of satisfying work. Moreover, since "labor-saving" devices are the proudest accomplishments of industrial Capitalism, labor itself is stamped with the mark of undesirability. But what is undesirable cannot confer dignity.

It is not merely that industrial Capitalism has produced forms of work both manual and white-collared, which are, as E. F. Schumacher says in his text *Good Work*, "utterly uninteresting and meaningless[, m]echanical, artificial, divorced from nature, utilizing only the smallest part of man's potential capacities, [sentencing] the great majority of workers to spending their working lives in a way which contains no worthy challenge, no stimulus to self-perfection, no chance of development, no element of Beauty, Truth, Goodness."[7]

Rather, Capitalism has so fundamentally alienated man from his own work that he no longer considers it his own. It is those with

---

[7] E.F. Schumacher, *Good Work* (New York: Harper and Row, 1979), p. 27.

the financial monopoly who determine what forms of work are to exist and which are "valuable" (i.e., useful for rendering profits to the owners of money). Since man spends most of his days working, his entire existence becomes hollowed out, serving a purpose which is not of his own choosing nor in accord with his final end.

In regard to the entire question of a "final end," if we are to consider Capitalism from a truly philosophical perspective, we must ask of it the most philosophical of questions: "Why?" What is the purpose for which all else is sacrificed, what is the purpose of continuous growth? Is it growth for growth's sake? With Capitalism, there is no "saturation point," no condition in which the masters of the system say that the continuous growth of corporate profits and the development of technological devices has ceased to serve the ultimate, or even the proximate, ends of mankind. Perhaps the most damning indictment of economic liberalism, indeed, of any form of liberalism, is its inability to answer the question "Why?"

Dr. Peter Chojnowski
Immaculate Conception Academy
December 28, 2003
Feast of the Holy Innocents

ARTHUR J. PENTY
His Life and Early Influences

ARTHUR JOSEPH PENTY was born in York, England, in 1875. His early education was interrupted in his thirteenth year, when, after continued marked success in his studies, he was put to work in his father's drawing office. Becoming adept in his craft concurred with a rather spasmodic interest in the cultural world around him. Architecture was his world, and the later years of his social and economic inquiries always evidenced the fact that planning and building soundly, constructively and permanently were part of his inner make-up. Factual observation was fundamental in his theory of knowledge and we are indebted to Stanley James's brief biography of him, written shortly after his death on January 19th, 1937, for a pointed reference in one of his books indicating his valuation of those gifted with a strong practical bent of mind.

Commenting on the great strides made in medieval times in experimental methodology in the physical sciences by the Franciscans, Penty had said:

> Learning being forbidden them by the rule of their order, they naturally acquired the invaluable habit of observing facts for themselves – a habit which book-learning is very apt to destroy. Men who begin life with much book-knowledge are very apt to look at things from the special angle provided by the books they have read and to neglect the lessons which the

* This chapter is taken from Rev. Edward J. Kiernan's Arthur J. Penty: His Contribution to Social Thought (Washington, D.C.: The Catholic University of America Press, 1941), pp. 1–12. Kiernan's work is a Ph.D. dissertation that was submitted to the Faculty of the School of Social Science of the Catholic University of America, supervised by Fr. John A. Ryan, and read by Prof. George T. Brown and Dr. Walter John Marx. Permission to reprint this excerpt was kindly granted by the Catholic University of America Press.

observation of facts can teach. It was thus that the Franciscans'
renunciation of learning stood them in good stead; it proved to
be the means whereby a new impulse was given to the acquisi-
tion of knowledge.†

Before he left York for London in 1902, his skill as an architect
was rather widely acknowledged. On several occasions his work had
received public commendation, and had been made the subject of a
monograph published in Germany.

Penty very shortly became affiliated with the Fabian Society
in London, whose members, including Sidney and Beatrice Webb,
Philip Snowden and George Bernard Shaw advocated a moderate
form of state socialism. Although he had some connections with the
Socialists in York, he had always been and was to the end of his life
a vigorous opponent of collectivism. Socialism in those days had a
rather loose significance, and anyone who was not in agreement
with the prevailing social and economic philosophy was liable to
term himself or be called a Socialist, as witnessed by the reception
given in some quarters to Pope Leo's encyclical on the condition of
labor. Penty preferred to call himself a radical Tory,‡ despite the
fact that all his friends told him the term did not mean anything.
He was associated with the Fabians until 1916 and, while he found
himself frequently at variance with many of the members, it gave
him the opportunity to develop his social thought and the vigorous
discussions, in which he never hesitated to participate, formed the
convictions which were later to be the basis for his constructive
plans for social reform. Quite logically and consistently the Fabians
favored the greater expansion of industrial power in order that the
descent to collectivism might be made the easier.*

It was during this period that Penty put out his first book, *The
Restoration of the Gild System*. The sources, as noted in the Preface of

---

† *A Guildsman's Interpretation of History* (London: George Allen & Unwin, Ltd.,
1920), pp 111–112; Stanley James, "Arthur J. Penty: Architect and Sociologist,"
American Review IX (April, 1937), p. 81.

‡ A somewhat similar antonymous designation – Tory Socialists – is used by Penty
in *Means and Ends* (London: Faber & Faber, Ltd., 1932, p. 113) for the branch of
the Conservative Party, followers of Disraeli, who repudiated the plutocratic domi-
nation of the party and from whom Penty expected the furtherance of constructive
social legislation.

* E.R. Pease, *History of the Fabian Society* (London: Fabian Society, 1925). The

that work, which influenced him in his antipathy toward the industrial arrangement of society, and which, together with his discoveries of the permanence of medieval architecture, turned his attention to the societal forms prevailing in that earlier age, were four writers who were vigorous participants in the nineteenth century aesthetic revolt against Industrialism. These four men were John Ruskin, Thomas Carlyle, Matthew Arnold and William Morris.†

Ruskin,[1] in particular, opposed the economic basis of the industrial system and excoriated it for its lack of understanding of human values and the disproportionate attention paid to material success. He deplored the existence of large scale production where it subordinated human labor to a cog in a machine and sublimated whatever creative and artistic instincts the workmen had. For Ruskin, the solution lay in the re-establishment of an economy similar to medieval times with regimentation of production and prices, and the organization of workers into groups resembling the craft guilds of those times.‡

Thomas Carlyle[2] was a sympathizer with the struggles of the working class in the industrial sections of England. He repudiated what he believed was the characteristic quality of the age: its selfishness, utilitarianism and materialism. Relations between employer and employee in his time were reduced to the terms of a wage bargain and were marked by the relative indifference of the former as to how the latter found the environment of his daily work or the conditions of his home life that were commensurate with the pay he received. Freedom was the abstract conception of the economic thinking of the age and of the political life of the times. But for the worker, servility was his status in the industrial world and his insignificant preference at the polls his only show of political freedom. Penty's dislike of democratic methods in the political sphere

Fabians were, however, opposed to Marx. They attacked his stand on class struggle as the instrument of reform, his economic interpretation of history and followed Jevons and the more orthodox economists on the subject of value. See *ibid.*, p. 238.

† *The Restoration of the Gild System* (London: Swan Sonnenschein & Co., Ltd., 1906), pp. vii, viii, 17.

‡ *Fors Clavigera* (New York: Merrill & Baker, n.d.), VIII, Letter 89, pp. 77–81; *Munera Pulveris* (Brentwood ed., New York: Merrill & Baker, n.d.), pp. 10–12; William S. Knickerbocker, *Creative Oxford* (Syracuse: University Press, 1925), pp. 150–161; D. Marshall, "War of the Machines," *Catholic World*, 145 (January, 1937), pp. 66ff.

was probably influenced to a great extent by Carlyle who preferred a government of the wisest, which was not always a consequence of popular preference in elections.†

The influence of Matthew Arnold's *Culture and Anarchy*[3] is cited as background reading in the earliest of Penty's writings. Though perhaps better known as one of those responsible for the introduction of the Hegelian idea of the State into England, he was a critic of the motivating forces in the industrial movement. The central idea of Arnold's teaching is the difference between means and ends, between machinery and the thing which it produces. In *Culture and Anarchy*, he set forth the idea that faith in machinery is a besetting danger and that the possibility exists in all ways of life to mistake means for real ends.‡

William Morris[4] was the originator of the Arts and Crafts Movement, and it attracted wide attention while succeeding in putting into practice hand production of such quality that reflected the craftsman's conception of beauty and perfection. The satisfaction which medieval workmen received in their work, despite the undeniable crudity and provincialism of their environment, was revived in these isolated instances. Morris felt that when the laborer was a craftsman only beautiful things were made, as reflected by the homes they dwelt in and the things they used for their personal needs. And these things were art since they embodied the visions of the workmen and expressed the composure and serenity of his labor. But in the modern industrial world, all this is changed. It is first of all characterized by its exterior ugliness. The worker, under no obligation to use his intelligence, is of economic value only insofar as he has physical strength or skill. Morris was not opposed to machinery in principle, but he, like Penty, undertook in his social thinking the means of restricting its use.*

Upon his return to England,[5] Penty renewed his acquaintanceship with A.R. Orage, who was also a member of the Fabians and interested in the Arts and Crafts Movement.

---

† Readings from "Past and Present" in *Social Reformers,* edited by Donald O. Wagner (New York: Macmillan Co., 1925), pp. 162–178; Frederick Roe, *Social Philosophy of Carlyle and Ruskin* (New York: Harcourt, Brace & Co., 1921).

‡ *Culture and Anarchy* (New York: Macmillan Co., 1902), pp. 113–129; Knicker-bocker, *op. cit.,* pp. 77–93, 128–149.

* *William Morris: A Selection from His Writings,* edited by Francis Watts Lee

Penty's dissatisfaction with the trend of Socialist thought and its complacency about the trends towards centralization of production was shared by Orage, who was a part owner of a weekly called *The New Age*. While somewhat less restrained than Penty in his enthusiasm for the adoption of medieval patterns in society, he saw in the rising strength of the trade unions a potential instrument in effecting industrial control. Contributors to his periodical included such names as Hilaire Belloc, Gilbert K. and Cecil Chesterton, H.G. Wells and George Bernard Shaw. *The New Age* advocated a "frank acceptance of the integral character of the unions and their right to an equal share in the responsibility of management in the business their members are engaged in," and went on to say that "the true line of development of the restoration of the essential features of the gild system, the responsibility of its members, the disposition of its collective forces and joint control of industry."†

Penty stressed the artistic and ethical implications in the guild doctrine while Orage was more concerned with seeking the sympathy and cooperation of the fast growing unions. H.G. Wells has said that Guild Socialism was the result of the impact of guilds and Mr. Penty on the uneasy conscience of Mr. Orage. A contributor to *The New Age*, S.G. Hobson launched the Guild Socialist movement with the publication of a book called *National Guilds*, a collection of periodical contributions edited by Orage, which went through three editions. Connected also with the Guild movement was one of the organizers of the Fabian Research Department, a brilliant intellectual named G.D.H. Cole who was a Fellow at Magdalen College, Oxford. The Guild movement appealed to him principally as a *via media* between collectivism and syndicalism.

The medieval guild had been an autonomous unit, local in character, but the tendency in the movement was towards a national guild. Penty's opposition was thereupon aroused as he contended the very evident possibility of over-centralization and the danger to personal freedom inherent in this policy. The champions of the national guilds, among whom was G.D.H. Cole and some

(New York: Humboldt Press, 1891), pp. 129–256. For Morris's influence on the whole Guild Socialist movement, see G. D. H. Cole, *Labour in the Commonwealth* (London: Commonwealth Press, n.d.), pp. 220–223. Also Niles Carpenter, *Guild Socialism* (New York: D. Appleton & Co., 1922), pp. 43, 46–47, 55.

† *The New Age*, Vol. 10 (January 18, 1912).

Oxford associates with Marxian sympathies, had stressed the fact that modern industry was on a national set-up with corresponding methods of efficiency in the way of purchasing and distributing that could not lightly be disregarded. Trade unions likewise were national and the thinking habits of their members were not provincial.†

The failure of the National Building Guild demonstrated the strength of Penty's position when it became evident that inefficient branches were retarding the efficient ones. Penty has outlined what were the basic differences between medieval and National Guildsmen:

> Local and national was not finally the issue that separated Guildsmen into rival groups, but different conceptions of the purpose of a Guild. Critics of National Guilds laboured under the disadvantage that the only term they had to describe the type of Guild they advocated was "Medieval Guild," and this term had a serious disadvantage.... We are indebted to Mrs Victor Branford for bringing this discussion at cross purposes to an end by designating the National Guilds as Producing Guilds and Medieval Guilds as Regulative Guilds, which does define the essential differences. For the essence of the National Guild is the organization of industry on an entirely self-governing basis, without any admixture of private interests for the purposes of production; while the essence of the Medieval Guild idea is a regulative body that does not propose to engage in production but to regulate it. The aim of such Regulative Guilds...being not primarily to supplant the individual producer by any form of co-operative production, but to accept the principle of the private management of industry for the present, at any rate, and to seek to superimpose over each trade or industry an organization to regulate its affairs in the same way that professional organizations enforce a discipline among their members today; with the difference that in addition to upholding a standard of professional conduct they would be concerned to promote a certain measure of economic equality among their members.
>
> The only difference between such Regulative Guilds and their Medieval prototypes would be that whereas the latter exercised control over employers and workers engaged in small workshops owned by small masters, the former would exercise

† Carpenter, *op. cit.*, pp. 164–165.

control over workers and employers engaged in large and small factories and workshops, owned by private individuals or limited liability companies or self-governing groups of workers (i.e. producing guilds or co-operative producers).†

Although the medieval implications of the movement seemed to fade after 1912, Penty still retained his interest in the movement and the preface to *Old Worlds for New* admitted the immediate impracticability of medieval guilds or regulative guilds as he later preferred to call them. Its practical application being temporarily thwarted, the medieval guild became for him the object of his long range policy. National Guilds had a purpose and an aim to secure the abolition of the wage system. He foresaw that workers in control of industry would find that there were underlying basic difficulties and contradictions in industrialism that would not be resolved by their attaining power. Their solution could only be effected by a return to local guilds and as a means to that end, Penty lent his approval to National Guilds.

Penty's first book, *The Restoration of the Gild System,* already mentioned, had appeared in 1906. It was a proposal for an alternative program of social reform to the Collectivists. He suggested concentration on five points:

1. The stimulation of right thinking upon social questions.
2. The restoration of a spirit of reverence for the past.
3. The dissemination of the principles of taste.
4. The teaching of elements of morality, especially in relation to commerce.
5. The insistence upon the necessity of personal sacrifice as a means to the salvation alike of the individual and of the State.

In 1917 appeared the second of Penty's works, *Old Worlds for New,* in which he foresaw the decline of Capitalism after the War and the inherent perils to the structure of society from the evils of mass production and fluctuating prices.

Guilds and the Social Crisis was written in 1919 and the same charges are reiterated with a growing concern at the wide divergence

---

† *Protection and the Social Problem* (London: Methuen & Co., Ltd., 1926), pp. 203–205.

of social and political views between the traditionalists on the one hand and the Marxians on the other.

Not satisfied with studying contemporary social phenomena, he evolved in *A Guildsman's Interpretation of History* the thesis that an historical consideration of the past presented in a sympathetic light and not in the light of materialist prejudices will lend a more rounded view to the aspect of industrialism and its consequences. This work, which exhibits the best efforts of Penty's scholarship, was finished in 1920 and had appeared serially in the columns of *The New Age* during the preceding year and a half. It was later translated into Japanese.

Guilds, Trade and Agriculture, written at a time when the Guild Socialist movement was in a transition stage, endeavours to elucidate Guild theory on the subject of exchange and in this work Penty regards the Guilds as a means to an end. This end is an establishment of a just price in marketable commodities. The necessary position of agriculture as a basic industry, which has been endangered by a policy of fluctuating prices, is viewed with concern, especially as affecting the future of England.

Post Industrialism, published in 1922, takes cognisance of the growing objection to enforced unemployment after the war, which took less of a transitory status than was hitherto conceded. The attack on mechanized industry had before come from two classes: those displaced by labor-saving devices who had to submit to all the inconveniences of a policy based on mobility of labor, and, secondly, from men like Ruskin and Morris, who had an aesthetic objection to the abuses of the machine.

In *Towards a Christian Sociology,* Penty applies the principles of Christian morality, as he views them, to the social and economic problems confronting society. The need of incorporating spiritual values in human relationships and the rescuing of human personality from the degrading level it had attained in modern industrial life is the theme of this book.

The crisis of unemployment and the necessity of establishing England as a self-supporting nation, once its supremacy as the workshop of the world had been seriously challenged, led him to collaborate with William Wright, a member of Parliament, in the writing of *Agriculture and the Unemployed,* a terse presentation of the issues involved and published in 1925.

The history of free trade with its unfulfilled promises of international amity and its depressing effect on national agriculture are given in *Protection and the Social Problem,* published in 1926.

Means and Ends summarizes the social philosophy of Penty, lays some emphasis on the false conception of the guild system as a necessarily lower stage in social evolution and is noteworthy for the first appearance of the principles which he establishes for the control of machinery, which are also included in an amplified form in his two succeeding volumes.

Communism and the Alternative, written for the Student Christian Movement, shows how Communism, in its glorification of industrialism and mechanistic processes and its promulgation of class war undermined its ulterior aim. The alternative theory proposed should rest upon the principles of Christianity and, unlike Communist theory, must accept human nature as it is found.

Tradition and Modernism in Politics, which is largely a series of articles originally appearing in the *American Review,* deals critically with Fascism, Communism, the Leisure State, the New Deal and the implications of his theories on money and machinery. Both this work and *Distributism: A Manifesto* were published posthumously in 1937. The latter was offered to the Distributist League subject to revision of any statements that possibly conflicted with the principles of that organization. Because of his death, the brochure was published without editing by the league.

In two articles appearing in *G.K.'s Weekly* in 1926, Penty had questioned his affiliation with the Distributist movement and had wondered whether he was entitled to call himself a Distributist. In these articles he outlines his social philosophy and invites comments on his theories from the Distributist side. He cites his earlier attraction for Socialism because it sought to replace competitive standards in society by co-operative or fraternal relationships. The moral impulse of the movement, he recognized as being incompatible with the more extreme economic reforms it advocated and his faith in Socialism was undermined. Guild Socialism presaged a brighter future, but where it succeeded there resulted a conciliation with and an advocacy of bureaucracy instead of its suppression.

With the Distributist program he differs on the position of property because under its aegis the restoration of private ownership is an end in itself. He says, "It is wrong to exalt private property as an ideal, but right to accept it as an expedient in view of the corruption of human nature." He stresses again the functional nature of property. Property has a social purpose because without it, activities necessary for the common welfare are unable to be properly fulfilled.†

Outright peasant proprietorship, he does not advocate because of the danger 1) of fostering the spirit of avarice, and 2) of the danger of the rich buying out the land from the poor and enslaving them. Instead he would vest ownership in the state, but its actual management would be in the hands of local autonomous bodies such as parishes or guilds, who would let these lands to groups or individuals responsible for their cultivation and who would be granted absolute security of tenure.

Objection was voiced by G.C. Heseltine in a later issue to Penty's land-holding plans. He maintained that "the security which is essential to every hard-working peasant and depends now on his own ability to make his holding yield a profit would be non-existent under any communal system." The local body, he considered an unwarranted infringement of the personal liberty of the land owner.‡

Penty, after considering the objections to his theories made by Heseltine and other Distributists, decided that in spite of resemblances, the differences between his view point and those of the Distributists were fundamental. He considers that they straddle the question of economic individualism, rejecting it in its larger aspects and restoring it in the form of peasant proprietorship. Liberty should be judged by its fruits in the same way that other ideas are judged and the fruits of liberty are evident to all. His chief objection to the Distributist program therefore revolves around the importance they give liberty in the restoration of property.* Chesterton and Belloc had been members of the Liberal Party in England, and Penty suspected a tinge of the old *laissez-faire* teaching in the Distributist movement. Penty, while not an authoritarian, believed more firmly in the restoration of authority and law to curb those who would take advantage of their position to defraud those in less secure stations.

---

† "Am I a Distributist?" *G.K.'s Weekly,* III (May 22 and 29, 1926). I: "Wanted: A Practical Policy," pp. 156ff; II: "Problem of Price," pp. 176ff.

‡ G.C. Heseltine, "Peasant Proprietorship," *G.K.'s Weekly,* III (July 17, 1926), p. 314.

* A.J. Penty, "The Answer is in the Negative," *G.K.'s Weekly,* III (August 14, 1926), p. 393.

It is, however, notable that in his later works Penty apparently abandoned his plan for parish holding of property, and quotes with approval in *Tradition and Modernism* the statement of Belloc that widely distributed property is necessary to human nature as a condition of freedom. Chesterton had accused Penty that he "was still full of that old Socialist idea of planning out the world from a criticism of the times." In 1937 Penty, to offset the idea, cites the futility of planning:

> The fallacy of planning is that it assumes society is static rather than dynamic. It seeks, as it were, to give permanence to what is after all only a phase of social development – to stabilize the abnormal. Planners skate about the surface, they are acutely conscious of the symptoms of the social disease, but are for the most part unaware of its nature.†

It is of particular interest to Catholic social students to examine the constructive criticism which Penty offers. Knowledge of the environment in which we live and of the traditions and culture which lie buried beneath its crass materialism is a prerequisite to the directive action which must, sooner or later, be undertaken. Practical measures can only be effective when the shallowness of mercenary motivations has been exposed along with immediate expediency as the criterion of social and economic value. "The whole power of evil," Penty points out, "rests ultimately upon its capacity to offer immediate advantages." There is no power on earth that will obstruct an individual in his rapaciousness and his selfishness unless he has a clear perception of his own spiritual end. And notwithstanding the fact that to the end of his life Penty had no religious affiliation, this man, surpassed in stature among the figures of the Anglo-Catholic[6] school perhaps only by Chesterton and Belloc, had this vision. "And so it is," he tells us, "unless people are willing to acknowledge and serve some higher principle than is dictated by their own appetites and desires, there can be for them no hope of social salvation."‡

---

† *Tradition and Modernism in Politics* (New York: Sheed & Ward, 1937), p. 181.

‡ *Towards a Christian Sociology* (London: George Allen & Unwin, Ltd., 1923), p. 45.

CURRENCY AND THE GUILDS
from *Towards a Christian Sociology*

I T IS A COMMONLY RECEIVED OPINION that gains some support
from the theory of Roman law that civilisation owes its existence
to the introduction of slavery. Such a view, however, is unten-
able. It receives no support from the actual facts, for we know that
slavery existed long before civilisation came into existence. Not
slavery, but the introduction of currency was the decisive factor in
the situation; and it is the failure to understand this fact that is one
of the root causes of confusion in social theory. It cannot fail to strike
the impartial observer as an extraordinary thing that currency, to the
introduction of which civilisation owes its very existence, should have
no recognised place in social theory. Yet such is the case. Its problems,
which are central in civilisation, are treated as the mere technical ones
of bankers and financiers, and are only approached from their point
of view. But the bankers' approach is most demonstrably a fundamentally false one; for it ignores the moral issue involved in the problem
of usury, and it is because the moral factor is ignored in discussion of
this problem that the whole subject is involved in such hopeless confusion. For currency, like every other social and economic problem,
to be intelligible must be approached historically, in the light of a
definite moral standard, and not as being a purely technical question
of men who are familiar with the intricacies of finance.

Currency was first introduced in the seventh century before
Christ, when the Lydian kings[7] introduced stamped bars of fixed
weight to replace the metal bars of unfixed weight which hitherto
had served as a medium of exchange. It was a simple device the consequences of which were entirely unforeseen; but the developments
that followed upon it were simply stupendous. It created an economic

* *This chapter originally appeared as Chapter XII of* Towards a Christian Sociology
(New York: The MacMillan Company, 1923), pp. 97–105.

revolution comparable only to that which followed the invention of the steam engine in more recent times. Civilisation – that is, the development of the material accessories of life – dates from that simple invention; for by facilitating exchange it made possible differentiation of occupation, specialisation in the crafts and arts, city life and foreign trade. But along with the undoubted advantages which a fixed currency brought with it, there came an evil unknown to primitive society – the economic problem. For the introduction of currency not only undermined the common life of the Mediterranean communities, but it brought into existence the problem of capitalism. And with capitalism there came the division of society into two distinct and hostile classes – the prosperous land-owners, merchants and money-lending class on the one hand, and the peasantry and debt slaves on the other, while incidentally it gave rise to the private ownership of land, which now for the first time could be bought and sold as a commodity.†

The reason for these developments is not far to seek. So long as the exchange was carried on by barter a natural limit was placed to the development of trade, because under such circumstances people would only exchange wares for their own personal use. Exchange would only be possible when each party to the bargain possessed some article of which the other party was in need. But with the introduction of currency circumstances changed, and for the first time in history there came into existence a class of men who bought and sold entirely for the purposes of gain. These merchants or middlemen became specialists in finance. They knew better than the peasantry the market value of things, and so they found little difficulty in taking advantage of them. Little by little they became rich and the peasantry their debtors. It is the same story wherever men are at liberty to speculate in values and exchange is unregulated – the distributor enslaves the producer. It happened in Greece, it happened in Rome, and it has happened everywhere in the modern world, for speculation in exchange brings in its train the same evils.

Though the Greeks and Romans thought a great deal about the economic problems that had followed the introduction of currency, to the end the problem eluded them. The ideal of Plato of rebuilding society anew on the principles of justice gave way to the

---

† See *The Greek Commonwealth*, by Alfred Zimmern, pp. 110–114.

more immediately practical aim of the Roman jurists of maintaining order. For, as I have previously pointed out, the maintenance of order rather than justice was the aim of Roman law, and as such it was an instrument for holding together a society that had been rendered unstable by the growth of capitalism. Thus we see there is a definite connection between the development of Roman civil law and the inability of antiquity to find a solution for the problems of currency. Freedom of exchange having led to capitalism, and capitalism to social disorders, Roman law stepped into the breach, and by legalising injustices sought to preserve order. And because of this, because of the generally received opinion in Rome that injustice was necessarily involved in the administration of the commonwealth, the jurists of the Antonine period came to postulate the Law of Nature in order to provide a philosophic basis for their legal measures of practical necessity. And as reform activities have ever since the Middle Ages been influenced by the Law of Nature, we see that the vicious circle in which they move owes its existence to the general failure to give to the problem of currency its position of central importance.

Unregulated currency gradually disintegrated the civilisations of Greece and Rome, and mankind had to wait until the Middle Ages before a solution was forthcoming, when it was provided by the Guilds in the light of the teaching of Christianity, though owing to the fact that the Guilds came into existence as spontaneous and instinctive creations of the people, their significance was entirely overlooked by Medieval thinkers, who, if orthodox, confined their social and political speculations to the range of issues covered by the Civil and Canon Laws, and, if revolutionary, to the issues raised by the Law of Nature, in neither of which systems Guilds found a place. This was one of the tragedies of the Middle Ages. For in organising the Guilds the townsmen of the Middle Ages unconsciously stumbled upon the solution of the problem of currency, but owing to the fact that the minds of thinkers and publicists of the time were engrossed with other things the social potentialities of this great discovery were lost to the world.

What then was the solution provided by the Guilds? It was to stabilise currency by the institution of a Just and Fixed Price. The Just Price had a central place in Medieval economic theory, though, strictly speaking, the Just Price is a moral rather than an economic idea. The Medievalists understood what we are only beginning to understand – that there is no such thing as a purely economic solution of the problems of society, since economics are not to be understood as a separate and detached science considered apart from morals. On the contrary, economic issues are primarily moral issues with economic equivalents. And for this reason Medievalists insisted upon things being bought and sold at a Just Price. They taught that to buy a thing for less or to sell a thing for more than its real value was in itself unallowable and unjust, and therefore sinful, though exceptional circumstances might at times make it permissible. The institution of buying and selling was established for the common advantage of mankind, but the ends of justice and equality were defeated if one party to any transaction received a price that was more and the other less than the article was worth.

This doctrine – that wares should be sold at a Just Price – together with another – that the taking of interest was sinful – was insisted upon by the Church, and obedience was enforced from the pulpit, in the confessional, and in the ecclesiastical courts. So effectively were these doctrines impressed upon the consciences of men that their principles found their way into all the secular legislation of the period, whether of Parliament, Guild or Municipality. The differing fortunes that followed these legislative attempts to secure obedience to the principle of the Just Price is instructive, for it demonstrates the undoubted superiority of the Guild as an instrument for the performance of economic functions. Parliament could do nothing but enact laws against profiteering, and as such its actions were negative and finally ineffective. But the Guilds were positive. They sought to give effect to the principle of the Just Price by making it at the same time a Fixed Price, and around this central idea there was gradually built up the wonderful system of the corporate life of the cities. Thus, in order to perform their economic functions, the Guilds had to be privileged bodies, having a complete monopoly of their trades over the area of a particular town or city; for only through the exercise of authority over its individual members could a Guild enforce a discipline. Profiteering and other trade abuses were ruthlessly suppressed; for the first offence a member was fined; the most severe penalty was expulsion from the Guild, when a man lost the privilege of following his trade or craft in his native city.

But a Just and Fixed Price cannot be maintained by moral action alone. If prices are to be fixed throughout industry, it can only be on the assumption that a standard of quality can be upheld. As a standard of quality cannot be defined in the terms of law, it is necessary, for the maintenance of a standard, to place authority in the hands of craftmasters, a consensus of whose opinion constitutes the final court of appeal. In order to ensure a supply of masters it is necessary to train apprentices, to regulate the size of the workshop, the hours of labour, the volume of production, and so forth; for only when attention is given to such matter is it possible "to ensure the permanency of practice and continuity of tradition, whereby alone the reputation of the Guild for honourable dealing and sound workmanship can be carried on from generation to generation," and conditions created favourable to the production of masters. Thus we see all the regulations – as indeed the whole hierarchy of the Guilds – arising out of the primary object of maintaining the Just Price.

But it will be said: If the Medieval Guilds were such excellent institutions, why did they disappear? The immediate cause is to be found in the fact that they were not co-extensive with society. The Guilds existed in the towns, but they never came into existence in the rural areas. That was the weak place in the Medieval economic armour; for it is obvious that if a Fixed Price was finally to be maintained anywhere, it would have to be maintained everywhere, both in town and country. That Guilds were never organised in rural areas is to be explained immediately by the fact that in the eleventh and twelfth centuries, when Guilds were organised in the towns, the agricultural population was organised under Feudalism, and money was only beginning to be used, so the problem was not pressing. But the ultimate reason is to be found in the fact that the impossibility of maintaining, in the long run, a Just Price that was not a Fixed Price was not at the time appreciated by the Church, which appears to have been blind to the need of Guild organization for its maintenance. Churchmen then thought, as so many do today, that the world can be redeemed by moral action alone, never realising that a high standard of commercial morality can only be maintained if organisations exist to suppress a lower one. Hence, it came about that, when in the thirteenth century the validity of the Just Price came to be challenged by the lawyers, who maintained the right of every man to make the best bargain he could for himself, the moral sanction on which the maintenance of the Just Price ultimately rested was undermined. Belief in it lost its hold on the country population, and then the Guild regulations came to be regarded as unnecessary restrictions on the freedom of the individual. Thus a way was opened in rural areas for the growth of capitalism and speculation, and this made it increasingly difficult for the Guilds to maintain fixed prices in the towns, until at last, in the sixteenth century, the whole system broke down amid the economic chaos that followed the suppression of the monasteries and the wholesale importation of gold from South America, which doubled prices all over Europe. It was because the Guilds were unable to perform any longer the functions that brought them into existence that they finally fell, and not because of the Chantries Act of 1547.[8] This Act did not attack the Guilds as economic organizations, as is commonly supposed, nor did it seek to confiscate the whole of their property, but only such part of their revenues as had already been devoted to specified religious purposes.

The explanation I have given of the decline of the Guilds is, so far as the details are concerned, the history of the decline of the English Guilds only. On the Continent, the decline pursued a different course, and as the factors in the situation were there much more complex, it is not so easy to generalise. Nevertheless, I think it is true to say that the ultimate cause of their decline is to be traced to the revival of Roman law. The Guilds went down not because they were unfitted by their nature to grapple with the problems of a wider social intercourse, as historians have too hastily assumed, but because the moral sanctions on which they rested had been completely undermined by the revival of a system of law that gave legal sanction to usury and permitted speculation in prices. Unfortunately, the truth of the matter, which is extremely simple, has been concealed from the public by a mysterious habit of economic historians of always talking about the growth of national industry, when what they really mean is the growth of capitalist industry. If they talked about the growth of capitalist industry, everyone would understand that the failure of the Guilds was a consequence of the moral failure of Medieval society, for the issues would be clear. But instead of talking about capitalist industry, they talk about national industry, and people are led to suppose that the Guilds declined because their type of organisation became obsolete, which is not the case as we shall later see.

MEANS AND ENDS
from *Means and Ends*

T HE FAILURE which must inevitably follow all attempts to find a solution of the social problem based upon the assumption that it is possible to stabilize the abnormal, must eventually bring people to see that a solution is only to be found in the direction of a return to the normal, and when that happens a new approach to the whole problem of social reconstruction will be become practical politics.

But what do we mean by returning to the normal? The best way of conveying to the reader what we mean is by telling him why modern society is to be regarded as abnormal. It is abnormal because material activities are overdeveloped, whilst spiritual ones carry on a precarious existence, because there is a lack of balance between the industrial and agricultural sides of society, because in a hundred directions personal and human ties are being dissolved and replaced by competition or the impersonal activities of the State. Looked at from this angle, modern society appears as an inverted pyramid in constant danger of toppling over, while reformers, blind to the peril, are engaged in widening the top, and still further restricting the base in the name of progress and evolution. Thus we see the problem of our civilization is a very different thing from that envisaged by the reform movement, inasmuch as the problem confronting us is not primarily a question of the redistribution of wealth, necessary as that may be, but of how to get the social pyramid to rest again foursquare upon its base instead of upon its apex, as it does at present.

* *This chapter originally appeared as Chapter II of* Means and Ends *(London: Faber & Faber, Ltd., 1932), pp. 53–92 It is here reprinted with the kind permission of Faber & Faber, Ltd., of London.*

It is to be affirmed that a society can only be in a stable and healthy condition when its manufactures rest on a foundation of agriculture and home-produced raw material and its commerce on a foundation of native manufacturers; and when its people share a common life in the family, the guild and locality. This is an ideal that can never be entirely attained in practice, except under the most primitive conditions; for no society can be entirely self-supporting according to the standards of civilization. Nevertheless, it is an ideal to be followed as closely as possible, since if this principle is disregarded a nation will tend to become economically and psychologically unstable. It will become economically unstable because, in proportion as the commerce and manufactures of a nation come to be dependent upon foreign markets and it comes to live upon imported foodstuffs, it will tend to find itself at the mercy of forces it cannot control; while it will become psychologically unstable because, insofar as the opposite ideal of cosmopolitanism comes to prevail, people become uprooted, and once they are uprooted they begin to find themselves at loose ends, which in turn undermines their moral and intellectual integrity, because on the one hand they find themselves released from social obligations, and on the other because they have no background of real experience by which to test the validity of ideas, and thus tend to become intellectually superficial and indifferent to moral values. In the past, the danger of cosmopolitanism was frankly recognized. Aristotle[9] and Aquinas[10] each desired to restrict foreign trade within the narrowest limits, because of the economic and moral disorders which they recognized followed in its wake, and the modern world supplies ample corroborative testimony of the truth of their contention. It is only when a people live a local life, are rooted in local traditions, that they develop character; and, I may add, it is only amid such local conditions of life and society that religion and art flourish, for it is only when the foundations of society are fixed, so to say, and where movement and flux are definitely limited, that the great traditions will take root.

If we accept normality as the ideal at which to aim, we inevitably come into collision with the idea of Progress and theories of social evolution as popularly understood because apart from the elementary needs of food, clothing, shelter and fuel they treat other human needs as non-essentials, subject to change and flux, on the assumption that human nature is capable of infinite adaptation to changing circumstances and without permanent needs. The essence of the idea of Progress is the belief that the new thing is to be preferred to the old. In consequence, it leads men to look with suspicion upon all traditions that have survived from the past, while it encourages an entirely uncritical attitude towards all developments. The future is featureless; to make it therefore the final court of appeal is to deny experience and to place ourselves at the mercy of every charlatan who comes along. There can be no way of exposing the fallacies involved in a new heresy, except by reference to some standard or experience in the past. The charlatan therefore, by appealing to the future while denying the past, discounts beforehand any possible criticism of his position, and cajoles the public into acquiescing in things they know to be wrong. Worst of all, belief in progress has silenced intelligent discussion of social and economic questions with the slogan "We can't go back," unmindful of the fact that history abounds in such returns. Nothing can be less intelligent than to object to any proposal on such grounds, for the implications of such a position are that the mistakes and follies of yesterday can serve as a foundation for the triumphs of tomorrow. No one but a fool in his private life acts upon such nonsense. If he makes a mistake he will seek to retrace his steps as quickly as possible. Yet what would be considered foolishness in private life is accepted in public life as the highest wisdom. But it won't appear wisdom much longer, for the choice that is being presented to us is between going back and going to the devil; and now that it has begun to assume this form, we shall doubtless agree to go back as the lesser of two evils. But it is not necessary for me to labour this point, for the process has already begun. The abandonment of the Gold Standard and the reversal of our Fiscal Policy demonstrate clearly that when the consequences of Progress become sufficiently serious we do not hesitate to "go back." But it is a pity that it should take a crisis of such magnitude to break the spell which the magic word Progress has imposed upon us.

Theories of Social Evolution provide a pseudo-scientific sanction to the idea of Progress. There are several such theories and as to some extent they cancel each other it will not be necessary to discuss them in detail separately. It will be sufficient to controvert a certain classification of history which is not only common to them all but has come to be used so far as I know by all economic historians, for to expose the fallacies involved in this classification is to knock the bottom out of the idea of Social Evolution.

According to this classification our industrial history is to be divided into four periods which are termed, respectively, the Family System, the Guild System, the Domestic System and the Factory System. These four systems are presented as four successive stages through which industry has passed in its evolution. It sounds plausible, but it is not true, for the four stages are not successive, inasmuch as the Domestic System does not develop out of the Guild System, but directly out of the Family System as did the Guild system; so that it is entirely wrong to speak of the Middle Ages as being characterized by the Guild System. On the contrary the Guild System and the Domestic System then existed side by side, one in the towns the other in rural areas, as two rival systems of industry with different moral intentions. The Guild System was a system of regulating industry to uphold a high standard of commercial morality and as such was communal in spirit, the legitimate successor of the Family System. The Domestic System on the contrary was a system of commercial exploitation and as such an illegitimate successor of the Family System which was communal in spirit. In other words, it was incipient capitalism and it happened that just as bad money drives good out of the market so the Domestic System, which was a morally bad system of industrial organization, undermined and eventually replaced the Guild System, which was a morally good system. To present therefore the Domestic System as the successor of the Guild System is as unscientific as it would be to present the boa-constrictor as the successor to the guinea-pig because he succeeds in eating him up. Yet economists who accept this classification and whose treatment of facts is entirely empirical claim to be scientific while they seek to dispose of any who see through the fallacies of their reasoning by designating them romantics.

When we come to the Factory System, we find the ground shifts again. I have in my possession a little book called *From Gild to Factory,*† in which this theory of economic history is summarized. But we cannot in any scientific sense speak of Guild to Factory, for a Guild is a system of industrial regulation whilst a factory is a system of industrial organization – two very different things. Consequently, while we might say "From Guilds to *laissez-faire,*" that is, from regulated to unregulated industry, or "From Small Workshops to Factories" which is from small to large units of industrial organization, we cannot say "From Guild to Factory" without confusing the categories of thought.

A further source of confusion arises from the custom of economic historians in speaking of the Guild System as local industry and the Domestic System as national industry, thereby leading people to suppose that the Guild System belongs to a lower stage of economic evolution, on the assumption that it is a system essentially limited in its possibilities, incapable of being given a national application, and therefore our interest in it can only be an antiquarian one. How baseless is this assumption is apparent when we reflect that if it were true it would mean that a system of industrial regulation, whose object was to uphold a high standard of commercial morality by the suppression of a lower one, could only be applied locally and that industry could only be organized on a national basis on the assumption that all attempts to uphold a high standard of commercial morality were abandoned. If such be the case – and it is the logical deduction from the position assumed by economic historians – then it may be asked on what grounds the supersession of local by national industry may claim to be a higher stage of industrial evolution?

Of course it is easy to understand why this kind of economic history became accepted as the truth. It justified modern civilization. It flattered the modern man who believes he is the last word in creation by suggesting that even the economic system of today is superior to anything that has gone before. Whether it will continue to flatter him much longer remains to be seen. Meanwhile this interpretation of economic history has been at the root of endless confusion of thought, and it is one of the reasons why now, when we are confronted by a national crisis, we are as a nation almost intellectually

† *From Gild to Factory,* by Alfred Milnes.[11]

bankrupt in the face of it. Further, it is to be said that Socialists only profess a belief in social evolution when it confirms their prejudices, for they are ready to throw it overboard when it does not suit their convenience. Thus they tell us that as a consequence of social and economic evolution the gulf between rich and poor has widened. If that is the correct interpretation of what has happened and if the division of society into rich and poor is brought about by evolution, then the only deduction to be made is that further evolution would separate them still more. But this is a conclusion which would not justify their political activities, so nothing is said about it.

To exorcize the bogies of progress and social evolution is a precedent condition of any intelligent discussion of the social problem and especially so in regard to the problem of machinery, for in no direction has belief in progress done more harm. In a sane and rational society, the use to which a force of such unknown potentialities as power-driven machinery should be put would have been a subject for serious deliberation. The discoveries in connection with it would have been followed by patient and exhaustive inquiry into their probable social and economic effects; and its use would, in the first instance, have been sanctioned in specific instances for experimental purposes only, while its social and economic reactions would have been very carefully watched; for though the undoubted advantages of machinery would have been recognized, society would not have deliberately closed its eyes to the perils which might follow the liberation of such an unknown power. Yet though the advance of machinery appears, in the early days of the Industrial Revolution, to have been viewed with some suspicion and hostility by the workers, because it threatened to displace their labour, no such apprehensions of danger appeared to have been felt by government and capitalists or by their henchmen, the economists; all of whom apparently took the unrestricted use of machinery for granted.

How are we to explain the blindness of society in the eighteenth century to the perils of the unrestricted use of machinery?—for at an earlier date it was different. Until the middle of the seventeenth century the efforts of the workers to resist mechanical innovations found support in high quarters. It is well known that the Tudors and the Stuarts were consistently opposed to the introduction of machinery which was injurious to handicraftsmen by creating unemployment, or would lower the standard of quality in the articles produced; and for a long time the opposition was successful in checking the mechanical tendency in industry. It was broken down eventually by the combined influence of two forces – the growth of foreign trade and Puritanism.[12] The discovery of America had provided England with an apparently inexhaustible market for its commodities. This fact, by dispelling the fear of unemployment which it was thought would follow the organization of industry on a quantitative basis, deprived the opposition to machinery of its strongest argument – the only one that would perhaps carry any weight with the middle class Puritans who were then becoming such a power in the land, and who joined with the landlords who had stolen the monastic lands to overthrow Charles in the Civil War. With the defeat of Charles[13] the old order came to an end and nothing henceforth stood in the way of industrial development and the enterprise of capitalists, who, incidentally, were invariably Puritans. The mind of the Puritan was hard and mechanical, devoid alike of any love of beauty or human sympathy. And once power passed into the hands of men of this calibre it is not surprising that any idea of restricting the use of machinery should have become anathema. To men so entirely destitute of any social or aesthetic sense, the idea of restriction was insufferable tyranny, a needless interference with personal liberty, and that was all there was to say about it.

And there was another reason for the blindness of society respecting machinery. In the eighteenth century the eternal validity of the theory of Natural Law was widely accepted as an indisputable scientific truth. According to this theory in the form it had then assumed, which incidentally was the theory behind Free Trade as originally understood, there is in society a power capable by its own internal volition of producing a social and economic equilibrium which would assert itself in proportion as governments abandoned all attempts to direct the course of social and economic development. Any restrictions to the use of machinery, therefore, were to be deprecated as other restrictions which limited natural activities were to be deprecated. It is probable that it was the influence of this theory that was decisive. For though it has entirely dropped out of political consciousness, its influence at the time was immense. It exercised an influence on European social and political thought from the fourteenth to the nineteenth century that is difficult to exaggerate, for during that period its sanction was sought for every idea of reform, while it was associated with every popular rising, from the Peasants' Revolt to the French Revolution. The fact, therefore, that the unrestricted use of machinery could be justified according to this theory must have turned the scales; for in spite of popular belief to the contrary, it is theories that rule the world and none are such humble slaves of them as the self-styled men of facts.

But the influence of the Law of Nature goes deeper, for not only was it decisive in changing the general attitude towards machinery, but it may be claimed that it was primarily responsible in effecting the transition from a social system organized more or less on a cooperative or corporative basis, in which the individual had a well defined status and security, to one in which he was left to fend for himself, to sink or swim as his own actions or circumstances might determine.

All this is admitted. But the real inwardness of the change and its bearing upon the present *impasse* are not understood. We have in the first place to take account of the fact that in the Middle Ages the individual enjoyed a definite status, whether under the Church, the Guild or Feudal System; he had security, he was cared for during sickness, provided for in his old age and was rarely troubled with unemployment. The result of this condition of things was that the Medieval man lived a comparatively care-free life. He was not beset with the anxieties that beset the man of today. The Middle Ages had drawbacks, but they were not the drawbacks of today; the things that were feared were not unemployment or destitution, but famine and pestilence which, when they came, visited all. But between times, economic historians are agreed, the Medieval man lived in rude plenty. He had plenty of the necessaries of life though luxuries were few. But that mattered little, for what we never experience we never miss.

A consequence of this condition of security was that the motives which today lead people to save or accumulate money were almost if not entirely absent. If the individual set out to make money it was not because considerations of prudence suggested his making provision for his old age or insuring against sickness or misfortune, but because he loved money, because he was avaricious. That explains why men who made the accumulation of wealth their primary aim in life were looked at askance in the Middle Ages and why trade and commerce were held in lower esteem than agriculture and craftsman-ship, as they are in China to this day. But when the corporate life of the Middle Ages was destroyed and the individual was left to fend for himself, the public attitude towards the individual who saved or accumulated money changed also; for under the new conditions, to save money did not bespeak a spirit of avarice, but was dictated by motives of common prudence. It was a social obligation, for not to save was not to make provision for sickness, old age or misfortune; it was to become a public charge. These changed circumstances bred a spirit of tolerance towards those who amassed wealth, lead-ing eventually to the acceptance of the rich as the natural leaders of society. And to what economic prudence suggested Puritanism gave religious sanction. The Old Testament taught that the virtuous man became materially prosperous, and the Puritans loudly proclaimed its truth. They came to believe that the virtuous inevitably became prosperous, and it was not long before the next step was taken – the prosperous were accepted as the virtuous, provided they did not inherit their wealth.

One result of this changed attitude towards money was that arts of life began to suffer. For when money is saved it is not spent, and it can be most easily saved by reducing expenditure on the arts which henceforth came to be regarded by the Puritans as needless luxuries, as inventions of the Devil. Thus the loss of status, by the stimulus it gave to saving, tended to promote a spirit of utilitarianism, which tendency was encouraged by corresponding changes that took place in the arts themselves. During the Middle Ages, the progress of taste had been from extreme simplicity to over-embellishment, but with the coming of the Renaissance reaction set in towards simplicity, which in the long run also moved towards utilitarianism. Whether this was finally due to the reaction of the spirit of Puritanism on the Arts or not must remain doubtful, for it can be explained entirely on aesthetic grounds. Among architects the decline is not connected with Puritan-ism, but with the pedantic tendencies of the Renaissance which ended in completely destroying the instinctive capacity of design which hitherto had been the common possession of the whole people. Yet Puritanism could not have been without its effect, for it is arguable that pedantry itself is a manifestation of the Puritan spirit because it is antipathetic to the spirit of spontaneity so essential to the arts.

To understand these things is essential to any understanding of industrialism; for it is to understand that it grew up in a spiritual vacuum, when all the great traditions were dead. It was this that gave industrialism its utilitarian, inhuman and anti-aesthetic spirit and explains why, in the long run, it is proving itself self-destructive. The total destruction of the balance between production and consumption which marks its present final stage is but the logical consequence of its exclusive preoccupation with means to the neglect, not to say contempt, for ends, which in turn is the consequence of the spirit of utilitarianism and the passion for investment and wealth-accumulation that Puritanism engendered.

Now that we have succeeded in diagnosing the disease, we are in a position to consider the remedy. As the present deadlock between production and consumption has come about as a result of an exclusive preoccupation with means to the neglect of ends, it follows that the remedy is to be found in restoring the balance by devoting ourselves to the furtherance of ends. This involves nothing less than a complete change in our attitude towards life – a change as complete as that which separates the spirit of Puritanism from that of the Middle Ages. We saw that the spirit behind industrialism was that of Puritanism. That spirit is now broken down. But though the human spirit has been liberated as a consequence of the decline of Puritanism it remains disembodied owing on the one hand to the absence of status and security which obliges people to think of money first, and the persistence of habits of thought and expenditure of Puritan origin which have survived its decay; and on the other because owing to a neglect of the arts it is unable to achieve legitimate expression. Such being the case we must aim on the one hand at regaining status and security for the individual, and on the other at the restoration of the arts to life by changing current habits of thought and expenditure. Let us consider these issues. It will be convenient to begin with the arts.

In schemes of reform, today, it is customary to stress the importance of encouraging science. Endowment of research has become an article of faith; as necessary to economic salvation. But science in industry is concerned with means rather than ends, and its encouragement can only intensify the competitive struggle. Meanwhile, the significance of art and its ability to restore the balance between means and ends is entirely overlooked. This would be excusable if the arts were still in the degraded condition they were in during the nineteenth century. But such is no longer the case. This century has seen a revival, a new renaissance of the arts – a renaissance in which this country has taken the lead. Architecture, painting, sculpture and crafts have, one by one, successfully emerged from their former degradation. And this revival, strange to say, has arisen amid the most adverse social and economic conditions; for it has coincided with an enormous contraction of art patronage. In spite of Puritanism and the general degradation of the arts during the last century, there yet remained a great deal of art patronage, even if it was not particularly well informed; but this last thirty years it has steadily contracted, owing on the one hand to the impoverishment of the old aristocracy, and on the other to the fact that the new rich prefer to spend their money on motorcars and antiques; while since the financial collapse in the autumn of 1929[14] the position has become desperate. That art survives at all is due to the fact that it is propped up by artificial means, to the fact that some artists have private means, and that there are positions for teachers. Surely, it is time we woke up to the actual situation, lest the revival should perish of neglect. If the arts should disappear, then, so far as I can see, our civilization must perish with them, for it is finally to art that we must look for correcting the balance between the means and ends of industry. If the arts were to perish, any hope of redeeming industry must also perish, for nothing then could prevent industrialism being carried to its logical conclusion. And the disease is, nowadays, sufficiently advanced for us to be able to imagine what that must mean.

Expenditure upon the crafts and arts is as necessary for our economic as for our spiritual salvation, for such expenditure acts like an economic safety-valve to prevent internal complications. Refusal to spend money on them on other things of permanent value is tantamount to sitting on the safety-valve, and it is because we have been sitting on it so long that things become so explosive. It is, I think, no exaggeration to say that there is no single thing which is responsible for the economic contraction that has taken place so much as the general unwillingness of people of all classes to spend money on the arts. In former times this was not the case. Expenditure upon the arts then was lavish. The great monuments of architecture bear witness to this, and it reacted to keep the economic arrangements of society in a healthy condition. And when I speak of the arts I must be understood to mean everything into which the aesthetic element enters, and this should be into everything that forms our environment, not only the fine arts of architecture (in the monumental sense), painting and sculpture, which most people think of in this connection. From the point of view of our economic redemption it is important that this restricted attitude towards art should be entirely broken down among the general public, as it has now for some time been in the art world, because until it is, it will be impossible to make much advance with the crafts. The patronage of the fine arts will always be confined to the rich and public bodies, whereas opportunities for patronizing the lesser arts and crafts are open to all, or were until industrialism destroyed our sense of values and provided so many ways for people to fritter away their incomes. It is especially important that people should be willing to spend sufficient money upon ordinary building, as to enable it to be done decently and to have done with the cheap-jack methods of building which have ruined our towns and country-side. It is safe to say that our old towns and villages would not command our admiration if those who had built them had approached the subject from the point of view of investments as is customary today. Building should be looked upon as a means of spending money; not as an investment. What it brings in as a return should be a secondary consideration, as it was in the past. It is interesting, in this connection, to observe that architectural opportunities today are for the most part confined to classes of building upon which returns are not expected, as is the case with churches, public and semi-public buildings. The exceptions are houses for the rich and commercial buildings erected for the purposes of prestige or advertisement. The latter motive, however, at times gives strange architectural results.

I said that expenditure upon the arts is like an economic safety-valve. It is important to understand exactly how this works. It is apparent that money that is spent upon goods for final consumption – in which category are to be included all art products – is money spent upon demand, whereas money which is invested in productive enterprises is money invested in supply. It follows from this, that if a balance is to be maintained between demand and supply, part of the national earnings should be spent upon goods for final consumption and part invested in productive enterprises; that is, part must be spent upon means and part upon ends, and both in their proper proportion. But when people become keen on making money they begin to spend less on goods for final consumption and to invest more in productive enterprises. A time comes when they lose all sense of proportion and when parrot-wise they recommend increased production as a remedy for all economic troubles. This upsets the balance between demand and supply, and intensifies competition. If they keep on investing their surplus income in new productive enterprises, the discrepancy between demand and supply will increase, until a situation is created like that today when every penny invested in new productive enterprises tends to increase unemployment; not to diminish it. For a long time the working of this simple law was, for us, obscured, because it was possible to us to dump our surplus products in foreign markets. But this is no longer possible because so many countries have taken to industrial production and supply their own needs. And so the truth is out at last. Production and consumption do not balance because people invest their surplus income in new industrial enterprises, and have lost the habit of spending money on goods for final consumption. People have done this in the expectation of increasing their wealth whereas, if they only knew it, they were really engaged in undermining the source of their incomes by bringing production to a standstill. "Governments," says Gustave Le Bon,[15] "are never overthrown. They commit suicide."

We have seen that the destruction of the balance between demand and supply, production and consumption, means and ends is due to the perfectly insane custom of re-investing surplus income in new productive enterprises for the purpose of further increase instead of spending it upon the arts and amenities of life. But I would not be so rash as to assert that the balance can nowadays be restored merely by advocating such expenditure, for habits are not to be changed in a day, and I fear the scales have been tipped too far to be capable of such a simple remedy. The average man today has his work set in trying to make ends meet. However desirous he might be of acting upon such advice, he does not find himself in a position to do so, while the rich as a class are unfortunately too inaccessible to ideas to be changed in a day; and the change would have to be made immediately and thoroughly if it were to be effective. The utmost, therefore, we may hope for in this connection is that the intelligent rich may be awakened to their responsibilities and be persuaded to spend their surpluses in such ways as to save the arts from destruction in the hostile economic environment in which they find themselves; to keep alive the flame of tradition until happier times return. For more, we shall have to wait until the majority are given security and status by being organized into Guilds, for not until they are given protection in this way can they have that relief from anxiety for the future which for them is a precedent condition of spending rather than investing any spare money they may possess. In the East, to this day, people with spare money spend it in art products. If you go into their houses you will find them full of expensive rugs, fabrics, metal and other craft-work. Judging by Western standards you might imagine such people to be very wealthy, but if you inquire you will find it is all they possess. These things represent their entire savings, which they sell in times of need. How much wiser this custom is than investing it in new productive enterprises, we are in these days beginning to find out. For not only do we find that as a result of this policy our cities and countryside are rendered ugly and abominable, but that our system of investments is, in the long run, proving itself to be self-destructive. Grasping at everything, we are ending in getting nothing. There is poetic justice after all.

To a generation like our own, which thinks in the terms of schemes and plans, this advice may appear unsatisfactory. But it is my contention that nothing less than a new dynamic, a new purpose, can lift us out of the trough into which we have fallen. Plans are necessary to enable us to carry on, and we shall require plans in the future if society is to be organized on a corporate basis, but for the present we must be content to plant a seed that will grow, for plans undertaken prematurely always produce results not intended by their authors. Before any plan for organizing society on a corporate basis can be successful, the spirit of the age must be changed; and this is just as true of the Labour and Socialist movements as of any other section of society. This century has witnessed a great emotional and moral revival. It is a consequence of the activities of the Socialist movement, to understand which it must be approached primarily as a moral revolt. The movement draws its recruits from among those who are outraged by the corruption and injustice of our economic system, and if we are to see in it its proper perspective this fact must never be lost sight of. Its great achievement is to have given the world a social conscience. If we compare the state of mind a hundred years ago, portrayed so vividly in the books of the Hammonds on the period covered by the Industrial Revolution; the callous, inhuman and hypocritical attitude of the rich towards the sufferings and misfortunes of the poor, and the prevailing hard, mechanical outlook on life and society with that which obtains today; the change of outlook and feeling is astonishing, amounting to nothing less than a revolution. And though we must not forget the many writers – Carlyle, Ruskin, Disraeli, Dickens, Charles Reade, Kingsley – who, by their writings, directed public attention to the injustices of our social system, I yet think the great change that has taken place is, in the main, due to the activities of Socialists, whose absolute devotion and untiring energy in the cause of the oppressed has made the social problem a living issue in politics, for the change is to be seen among people entirely unaffected by Socialist theories. But though moral and emotional values have changed, spiritual, aesthetic and intellectual ones have not to an equal extent, for the mass of people still accept the quantitative and utilitarian standards of industrialism, unaware that any conflict exists between them and their emotional and moral impulses; though the practical failure of Socialist measures, based upon the assumption that the quantitative standard is above suspicion, should have brought that home to them. In these circumstances, it is evident that before any schemes for organizing society on a corporate basis can meet with success, the people must be given new spiritual, aesthetic and intellectual values. They must, in a word, be born again. They must be awakened to a new conception of the social problem, which sees the economic problem not as a detached issue, but as the more obtrusive symptom of an internal spiritual disease; for though the situation being what it is, it is natural for reformers to be primarily concerned with the solution of the economic problem, yet it is to be affirmed that they never will find a solution for it until they come to search for it in the light of spiritual truth instead of the materialist philosophy.

The helplessness of statesmen and reformers in facing the problems of machinery and rationalization should bring home to all the inadequacy of the quantitative and utilitarian point of view. Machinery today is displacing labour at an alarming rate. Yet neither statesmen nor reformers demand its regulation. On the contrary, they tell us that "they do not seek to go back to Ludditism;[16] that rationalization cannot be stopped for we must have efficiency and develop our economic resources." Why is this? It is because any proposal to restrict the use of machinery is sheer obscurantism to men who accept the materialist philosophy. It is sinning against the light. And so though they recognize that machinery is creating unemployment and will increasingly create it, yet because of their limited vision they are unwilling to entertain the idea of restricting its use. And so it must be until they are born again, until they come into possession of spiritual truth; for not until they come into possession of higher values with which the unrestricted use of machinery conflicts will they be able to see that to restrict its use is not obscurantism but the highest wisdom. And this is one of the reasons why the revival of the arts is a precedent condition of social salvation. Art is one of the approaches to spiritual truth.

When people do awaken aesthetically, they come to see that the Qualitative Standard of the arts inevitably conflicts with the Quantitative Standard of industrialism. It comes about this way. If you produce in quantities you must, if you are to sell your products, take the world as you find it. You must accept the taste and standards of the average man at any given moment as your standard. From this it follows that you exclude everything that is above the average. You begin by excluding standards of taste that are above the average and you end by excluding men who are above the average. But to exclude everything that is above the average is to exclude the best men and things. And this, in the long run, is fatal to society, for unless average men are in contact with persons and things higher than themselves, they tend, progressively, to degenerate. Society loses its salt by being deprived of true leadership, and because of this the theory of averages in industry, as in politics, leads ever to a lower level.

To attack the Quantitative Standard is to attack the philosophy underlying machine production which has led to its abuse. But though such an attack would bring into existence an atmosphere in which proposals for a limitation of the use of machinery would be listened to, it yet does not of itself provide any principle for its regulation. On the contrary, it is only when we approach the problem in the light of the Qualitative Standard that principles for the control of machinery can be formulated. The following occur to me:

(1) The use of machinery should be restricted where its use conflicts with the claims of personality – that is, it should not be allowed to turn men into robots.

(2) It should not be allowed where its use is injurious to health.

(3) It should not be allowed to create economic disorders like unemployment.

(4) It should not be allowed where it conflicts with the claims of the crafts and arts.

(5) It should not be allowed to multiply commodities beyond the point at which natural demand is satisfied – that is, beyond the point at which sales need to be artificially stimulated by advertisement.

(6) It should not be allowed to trespass seriously upon the world's supply of irreplaceable raw material.

The enforcement of these regulations would I imagine abolish most of our machinery; and to the remainder, there could be no objection, for limited to this extent we might breath freely again, and forget what a menace machinery had ever been to the world. We should certainly be better off spiritually, and I do not hesitate to say that most people would be better off materially though it is not so easily proved. Nevertheless, it is only necessary to have a slight acquaintance with our industrial system to realize that in the main machinery today is not used for the production of wealth, but for the production of illth. Since the introduction of machinery the labour of the community has been increasingly misapplied with the result that only a very small percentage of our industrial activities are devoted to the production of wealth. The rest is devoted to the production of rubbish or waste of one kind or another. It runs to waste in the production of armaments, on cross distribution, advertisements, needless selling and advertising costs and in other ways. Well has it been said that our high standard of living is not really a high standard of living at all, but a high standard of wasting. It is significant that while the productive capacity of industry has doubled or trebled during this century the cost of living is very much higher today than it was in the year 1900. There is only one explanation for this. Our greatly increased production capacity has been used not to increase wealth but wasted on competitive selling, cross distribution and armaments.

Where machinery can be used to produce goods in large quantities the saving in the cost of production is enormous. But it is important to recognize that the costs of distribution are at the same time enormously increased, for when goods are produced in great quantities they cannot be disposed of locally, and great selling and advertising organizations are brought into existence to dispose of them. An American economist, Mr. Stuart Chase,[17] has shown how as a result of mass production, the selling costs have been increased so enormously that it not infrequently happens that in the end the public have to pay more for commodities made by mass production than if they had been made by hand.† It might be supposed, if such be the case, that when the costs of distribution increased the selling costs of machine-made goods beyond a certain point, handicraft would return as a consequence of the normal operations of supply and demand. But this cannot happen so long as large-scale industry continues to function, because under the new economic conditions that have been brought into existence the craftsman finds that he cannot escape high selling costs. For this reason handicraft today is

---

† *Your Money's Worth,* by Stuart Chase. The MacMillan Company, New York.

infinitely more expensive than it would be under normal economic conditions. But if normal economic conditions could be restored it would be found that the discrepancy in price between hand- and machine-made goods would not be so great, while in many cases hand-made goods would be cheaper.

In any comparison between the relative advantage of machine and hand production the fact should not be lost sight of that machine production entails an enormous number of expenses which hand production under more primitive economic conditions escapes. In an interesting book, *Economics of Khaddar*,† Mr. Richard B. Gregg[18] inquires into the economic prospects of the Gandhi movement in India. He tells us that if the efficiency of the spinning wheel could be increased two and a half times and the hand loom ten times they would stand even with power-driven machinery because of the enormous number of expenses which hand production escapes, and it is not improbable that invention may be able so to increase the efficiency of hand weaving as to make them level since already it has done a great deal to fill up the gap. Mr Gregg summarizes the costs which hand-produced cotton goods using locally produced material and selling locally escape under 25 headings as follows:

(*a*) SAVINGS IN COST

Elimination or great reduction of existing cost due to:

1. Assembly of raw material.
2. Storage of raw material.
3. Railway and steamship transportation.
4. Baling or packaging required by long transportation.
5. Injuring and wasting of cotton fibre by high-speed power ginning and carding.
6. Injury of cotton seed by such gins and mixture of seeds of different strain and grades.
7. Certain steps in processing, rendered necessary by condition of material as a result of large-scale assembly, long-time storage in bales, long transportation;

---

† *Economics of Khaddar*, by Richard B. Gregg, pp. 79, 83. S. Ganesan. Triplicane, Madras, S.E.

e.g., opening of bales, removing impurities, removing adverse effects of compression, etc.

8. Irremediable damage from transportation, storage and large-scale handling.
9. Fire and theft insurance on materials and products.
10. Storage of completed product.
11. Advertising.
12. Obsolescence of product due to changes of taste and fashion.
13. Money, labour, land, fuel and other facilities and materials being wasted or diverted into luxury production.
14. Brokers' "wholesalers," commission-men's and other handlers' and middlemen's charges and profits.
15. Fluctuations in price of both raw material and finished product: also speculation therein.
16. Overhead costs arising from:
    (a) large clerical and sales forces;
    (b) expensive machinery, buildings, land and other equipment.
17. Fuel and power charges.
18. Legal expenses.
19. Bankers' charges for loans, discounts, etc.
20. Income and super taxes.
21. Municipal taxes and water rates.
22. Repair and maintenance of machinery and buildings.
23. Depreciation and obsolescence of machinery, boilers, builders and equipment.
24. Workmen's compensation insurance or legal damages to injured employees.
25. Fire insurance on buildings and machinery.

He further adds:

(b) REDUCTION OR ELIMINATION OF RISKS DUE TO:

1. Famine or crop failures.
2. Fire.
3. Theft.

4. Strikes or lockouts.
5. Transportation delays.

(c) INDIRECT EFFECTS OR CONCOMITANTS ECONOMIC AND SOCIAL

1. Reduction in cost of living as a result of lightening the burden listed under (a).
2. Greater freedom from foreign financial and commercial interests and control.
3. Improvement of quality of product in respect to durability, adaptability to use and beauty.
4. Reduction of social evils such as slums of cities, physical and moral deterioration due to city life, unemployment and its fears and moral degeneration.
5. Decrease of tendency to urbanization and consequent reduction of national expense for railways, municipal works etc.
6. Reduction of power of financiers, large and small, over the lives of the people.
7. As one element of 6, a reduction in the amount of credit and credit instruments needed in trade, and hence a check on the inflation of credit and private and irresponsible control of credit with its consequent rises in prices.
8. More leisure.
9. More health and bodily and mental energy.
10. Enhancement of creative motives and a reduction of the opportunities and temptation for acquisitiveness, greed and imperialism.
11. The release, for purposes of growing food, of excess land now used for cotton growing.

Some of these items appear to be duplicated, but there are important omissions. We may add:

1. A more diffused prosperity; for machine production by concentrating power in the hands of a few enables the few to exploit the many.
2. Cost of maintenance of the unemployed.

3. Economic instability due to machinery as a disturbing factor.
4. Reduction of the danger of war by eliminating the struggle for markets and raw materials which under industrialism has been such a fruitful cause of wars.
5. National savings on cost of armaments and reduction of military establishments in peace times.

Now there is no branch of industry in which the discrepancy between hand and machine production is greater than in that of textiles. If therefore when everything is taken into account the saving effected by machinery is so small, how much less will it be in other crafts which do not lend themselves so readily to machine production? For these reasons, I am of the opinion that if the use of machinery was restricted to its legitimate province and used only on a limited scale we should be better off, because as in that case it could be reconciled with local markets, we should benefit by its advantages whilst escaping the heavy liabilities which are the inevitable accompaniment of large-scale production and de-localized markets.

But, I shall be told, all this sounds very nice but it has no relevance to practical politics; it is too remote. Yet it is not as remote as might at first sight appear. It may be true that politics are concerned more with appearances than with realities, yet in times of crisis appearances and realities coincide and the trend of events is to bring them together. May we then not assume that the day is not far distant when politics will have no option but to deal with realities, and when that day comes ideas will be considered which in the meantime would not be listened to? Our industrial system is slowing down and unless a break is made with the ideas that govern politics and industry it will certainly come to a standstill. Therefore it is not unreasonable to suppose that the idea of restricting the use of machinery may enter practical politics, for when people see what social and economic disaster follows its unrestricted use they may become reconciled to the idea of restricting it.

REGULATIVE AND PRODUCING GUILDS
from *Towards a Christian Sociology*

I F THE CENTRE OF GRAVITY of the economic problem is to be found in currency and price rather than in property, every other problem in society will assume a different perspective – questions which nowadays are regarded as issues of primary and fundamental importance will be relegated to a secondary position, while issues that hitherto have been treated as secondary and unimportant will become matters of primary interest.

In this process of transformation our conception of the nature and purpose of the Guild will be completely changed, inasmuch as regulation rather than production will now become its primary aim. Producing Guilds have hitherto found favour among Socialists because they recommended themselves as instruments for the abolition of the private ownership of property, the substitution of workers' control for private management being considered a means towards this end. But once it is recognised that the centre of economic gravity is to be found in currency and price rather than in property, a different type of Guild will find favour, since from this point of view the primary aim of Guild activity is the regulation of prices, and the type of Guild best adapted to perform this function is not the producing but the Medieval or Regulative type, which would superimpose over each industry an organisation to regulate its affairs much in the same way that professional societies enforce a discipline among their members, with the difference that, in addition to upholding a standard of professional conduct, such Guilds would be concerned to promote a certain measure of economic equality among their members, in the same way that trade unions do today. Such guilds would insist that

* *This chapter originally appeared as Chapter XV of* Towards a Christian Sociology *(New York: The MacMillan Company, 1923), pp. 134–144.*

all who were engaged in any industry should conform to its regulations, which would be concerned with such things as the maintenance of Just and Fixed Prices and rates of wages, the regulation of machinery and apprenticeship, the upholding of a standard of quality in production, the prevention of adulteration and bad workmanship, mutual aid, and other matters appertaining to the conduct of industry and the personal welfare of its members.

Though such Regulative Guilds are identical in principle with the Medieval Guilds, there is yet no technical difficulty that stands in the way of their establishment over industry today; for the principles to which it is proposed they should give practical application are finally nothing more than the enforcement of moral standards. For though modern industry differs from Medieval industry, the differences are technical, and no technical difference can involve a difference of moral principles. On the contrary, what is involved is a difference in application, inasmuch as whereas the Medieval Guilds only exercised control over employers and their assistants engaged in small workshops and owned by small masters, our proposed modern Regulative Guilds would exercise control over employers and workers engaged in both large and small factories and workshops owned by private individuals, joint-stock companies and self-governing groups of workers. To make such control effective, it would be necessary to depart from the rules of the Medieval Guilds to the extent that authority would have to be invested in the whole body of members – employers and workers – instead of being exclusively in the hands of the masters, as was the case in the Middle Ages. For the typical employer today is not a master of his craft, who is jealous for its honour, as was the Medieval employer, but a financier who is only interested in the profit and loss account, and therefore is not to be trusted with final authority. Hence the conclusion that if any standards of honesty and fair dealing are to be upheld, prices and wages fixed on a basis of justice, machinery and other things necessary to the proper conduct of industry to be regulated, the final authority must be vested in the trade as a whole, for only those who suffer from the growth of abuses can be relied upon to take measures to suppress them.†

---

† Such a conception of industrial reorganisation is not as remote from practical politics as many will assume, for the scheme of industrial reorganisation (*cont'd*)

In comparison with the enforcement of such moral standards over industry, all other issues, such as whether the workers are to be engaged in co-operative production or Producing Guilds, whether they have small workshops of their own or are employed by others, are secondary. They are not matters of principle, but of expediency or personal preference. There is no greater mistake than to suppose that every man would prefer to work co-operatively with others. On the contrary, the majority – the vast majority, I believe – would, other things being equal, prefer to be employers or employed. Any number of men prefer to work as assistants because they don't like responsibility, while there are numbers of men of a masterful disposition, who are too individualistic by temperament to love co-operation, and who would be mere grit and friction inside any organisation on a co-operative basis, while again it is to be observed that there are many men who prefer to work under such men of a masterful disposition because they like to know just where they are, and others prefer to work alone. Preferences of this kind have nothing to do with indifference to or love of money. Men may be any of these things and be good or bad citizens; it is entirely a question of differences of temperament. For this reason a mixed economy which is flexible and contains different types of organisation is best adapted to differing human needs and the varied circumstances of industry. What is important is that these various types of men in any single industry – employers, employed, co-operators – should submit to the same statutes and regulations or suffer expulsion. If moral standards are enforced over industry by Regulative Guilds the particular way men prefer to work or organise could be left to themselves to decide, for their differences could have no harmful consequences; while it is to be observed the enforcement of the Guild discipline would tend to weed out undesirable forms of industrial organisation, such as limited liability companies.

Such then is our conception of the primary purpose of Guild organisation. But it is not on this basis that the Guild idea has hitherto been promoted in this country. On the contrary, approaching

---

proposed in the Majority Report of the Industrial Council of the Building Industry (better known as the Building Trades' Parliament) proceeds upon such a basis. It is a remarkable testimony to the truth and universality of Medieval principles that its promoters were unaware of its likeness to Medieval organisation.

An account of it is to be found in my *Post-Industrialism* (Allen & Unwin).

the problem of Guild organisation from the point of view of property rather than currency and price regulation, the Guild idea became identified with that of co-operative production or Producing Guilds; for National Guilds was an attempt to give universal application to a principle of organisation that on a small scale was practised with success under the auspices of the co-operative movement by giving it a base in the Trade Unions, and it would have cleared the air of a great deal of discussion at cross purposes if from the first they had been called Producing Guilds instead of National Guilds; for it is not the Guild idea in the larger sense as expressed in the Regulative Guild or even the Producing Guilds that is finally called in question by the failure of the Building Guilds, but the particular policy and form of organisation popularised by the National Guilds League, as nowadays its members are prepared to admit. National Guilds, as we have always insisted, were a compromise, and a compromise that could not last, for it was compounded of incompatibilities. So far, therefore, from the failure of the Building Guilds heralding the defeat of the Guild idea, it should by exposing the inconsistency of the National Guild position, prepare the way for its acceptance. For it has not been the Medieval elements in Guild theory that have been found wanting in practice, but the modernist ones that it borrowed from Collectivism.

Meanwhile it will be interesting to compare the Building Guild experiment with the Italian Producing Guilds,† for the failure of the one and the success of the other may suggest to us the lines upon which a new policy for Producing Guilds should be based. In this connection the first great difference that we notice is that, compared with the Italian Guilds, our Building Guilds were exotic. They were created artificially from above to execute the housing schemes and developed with such rapidity as to engender all the defects and shortcomings which everywhere accompany organisations of mushroom growth. For their difficulty of obtaining credit, which was the immediate cause of failure, and the internal problem of organisation which, apart from the problem of credit, must eventually have resulted in failure, were both largely the result of a too rapid

---

† My information on Italian Guilds in based upon *Guilds and Co-operatives in Italy*, by Odon Por, translation by E. Townshend (Labour Publishing Company), and a correspondence with the author.

growth; for when growth is too rapid, organisations do not grow up in an organic way, and suffer in consequence from a multitude of maladjustments which, leading to confusion and dissensions, are apt to prove disruptive.

In Italy the development was different. The Producing Guilds there originated, as did the smaller Producing Guilds in this country which came into existence as a result of the boom of the Building Guilds, to provide work for the unemployed, and their development in the early stages was very slow indeed, for it should be known the Italian Building Guilds are already sixty years old. Thus it was, instead of being promoted from above, they began at the very bottom of things – often as mere organisations of labour undertaking simple work such as navvying, where "labour" is the most expensive "raw material." From such humble beginnings, they gradually advanced step by step, consolidating their position as they went on, until they could undertake works of importance where more plant and capital was required. And because they grew up slowly in this unobtrusive way they were never seriously perplexed by the problem of credit on the one hand nor with difficulties of internal organisation on the other, while the fact that at the beginning they had no idea of creating a new social order, no other aim in fact than to provide work for the unemployed, any working theory that they have come to possess has been the result of experience and not the result of any *a priori* reasonings, for any other "ism" – Socialism, Syndicalism or Fascism – with which any of the Guilds may be identified today has been grafted onto them since, and had nothing to do with their origin.

To understand this is important. For the immunity of the Italian Guilds in their early stages of development from the disruptive influence of Socialist theories led them to adopt a commonsense attitude towards the problems confronting them which might otherwise have been impossible. The Italian Guildsmen began by accepting the fact that the Guilds they organised had to function within the capitalist system and be as businesslike as any private firm, and did not therefore attempt to push the principles of democratic control so far as to make such functioning impossible. For when such principles are pushed too far, as it is in National Guild theory, the rank and file inevitably come into collision with the administrative staff, into whose hands decision as to details inevitably falls, for there is a limit to the number of things to which committees can attend. The non-recognition of this fact was a constant source of friction in the Building Guilds. Their ideal was to be democratic from the top to the bottom, and this led to an extraordinary multiplicity of committees, which made the organisation of the whole of industry upon such a basis a proposition entirely unthinkable.† He maintains that the successful committees he has known have been consultative and the failures executive. Experience was to prove that on the ultra-democratic basis upon which they were organised there was no discoverable basis of co-operation between the administrative staff and the rank and file; a fact which came very much in evidence every time a new appointment was to be made. And this difficulty inherent in National Guild theory was further complicated by the fact that the rapid growth of the Building Guilds necessitated the recruitment of their administrative staffs from the middle class instead of from the rank and file as was possible in Italy, because of their slower growth, and this, because it involved differences in economic status, naturally led to dissatisfaction in an organisation that came into existence to promote economic equality.

The different standards of living of the working and middle classes is a real obstacle in the path of their close co-operation in any organisation that is democratically controlled. For though the middle-class Socialist when he preaches economic equality means that with a better distribution of wealth the working class would be raised up to his own standard of living, the idea is interpreted by the working-class man as meaning that the middle-class man should be prepared to accept the same wage or salary as himself. And this constitutes a real difficulty that should be faced. It is to be traced to the fatal habit of reformers of exalting a standard of idealism which they personally are not prepared to act upon. It borders on insincerity, for I do not think the middle-class Socialist has any right to ask the working class to live up to a standard of social idealism that he is not prepared to live up to himself. Yet it seems to me that this is what happened under the Building Guilds; for while the working-class member was asked to work at a standard rate and forego any share in any profits that he might help to produce, the middle-class man

---

† In *Psychology and Politics* Dr. W. H. R. Rivers argues that committees should be consultative rather than executive.

expected to take his share out in the form of a higher salary. Much of the demoralisation that overtook the Building Guild was, I am persuaded, traceable to this fact, for it was much talked about. It seems to me if wages and salaries are not to be equal, it would be wiser to allow the workers to have a share in the profits, as is the case with Producers' Co-operatives. I say it is the wiser thing – I should say, I think it is the only thing – to do, if disaster is not going to follow disaster. And I can see no objection to it. For if we had Regulative Guilds, that would maintain just and fixed prices and wages and other matters relating to the conduct of industry, such Producing Guilds could not degenerate into capitalist concerns, for all the distribution of such profits would mean would be that men were rewarded for any extra exertion they might put into their work, and this would provide the incentive that is required to keep up the morale of the Guild. This, I submit, is only common sense. The men in the Building Guild worked hard at the beginning. But after a twelve-month, when the wave of enthusiasm had spent itself, there came the inevitable reaction which always follows the attempt to live up to an idealism pitched in too high a key. Of course Socialists are led into this error by their belief in the natural perfection of mankind, whereas the fact is most demonstrable that all men are sinners.

I do not know if a time will ever come when the whole of industry will be organised in local Producing Guilds under the control of National Regulative Guilds, but if it did it might prove to be a misfortune, the prelude of decline, for if private management were entirely to disappear I cannot help thinking that initiative would disappear with it. It would disappear under Producing Guilds as it is disappearing under limited liability companies, and for precisely the same reason – that as the majority of men lack imagination, they are only willing to adopt any new idea when it has been proved to them by demonstration, and as it is for this reason invariably impossible to get any committee to back any new idea from the start, it follows that new developments are only possible on the assumption that private industry is not entirely extinguished. The entire disappearance of private industry would certainly place an insuperable obstacle in the path of the revival of the crafts and arts. "Economic co-operation," says Dr. Jacks,[19] "runs to quantity, because quantity is something that can be proved to everybody's satisfaction; meanwhile quality, which is incapable of proof, is apt to suffer."† I am not quite sure whether this will always be true, but it is certainly true today – at any rate as far as the crafts and arts are concerned – for it seems to be absolutely impossible to forge any permanent link between them and any form of collective activity at the present time, in spite of the constant efforts that are made to overcome the difficulty. It may be argued that if Regulative Guilds were established and prices fixed, the difficulty would disappear. But I am not quite sure whether such would be the case, for the difficulty is psychological as well as economic, and it is possible that if the economic difficulty were removed the psychological difficulty would remain, because in the absence of private industry the more enlightened minority would be powerless against the blind majority into whose hands the control of administrative machinery would fall. Viewed in this light, the problem of the arts presents itself finally not as a problem of taste but of power. It is the problem of keeping open an avenue for their revival, and my fear is that if Producing Guilds become too widely established before the arts are revived all such avenues would be finally closed. For if bad traditions of design and workmanship once get into such guilds, as seems inevitable today, there will be no getting them out again apart from outside influence. This is one of the many reasons why I feel that Regulative Guilds should come first.

---

† *From the Human End,* by L.P. Jacks.

THE ETHICS OF CONSUMPTION
from *Old Worlds for New: a Study of the Post-Industrial State*

I F THERE IS ONE THING more than another which the experience
of the Arts and Crafts Movement has proved conclusively, it is
the impossibility of any group of craftsmen, however gifted – and
in this connection it is well to remember that the movement secured
the active support of the cleverest architects and artists of its day – to
effect any widespread reform, apart from the organized support of the
public. Without a propaganda movement to teach the public, the craftsman found himself very much at the mercy of the existing demand. A
German poet[20] has said that "against stupidity even the gods fight in
vain," and on the aesthetic side of things the British public is peculiarly
stupid. It utterly fails, for the most part, to understand the meaning
and purpose of art. It fails to realize that beauty and sweetness are
essential elements of any human perfection, and that art, when it is
vital, enters into every operation of industry, from the making of bricks
to the highest flights of the imagination. It conceives of art as a veneer
or decoration superimposed upon, or added to something which would
otherwise be ugly. The idea that art is organic and inherent in the
nature of a thing from the moment of its inception has never so much
as entered the public mind. And yet it is precisely the perception of this
truth which is the essence of the artist. He recognizes that there is a
right way of doing everything, and that right way is art.

The ordinary British philistine will not admit this. Being without the finer aesthetic perceptions, which alone can enable a man to
determine which is the right way of doing things, and lacking that
spirit of humility which in the ages of great traditions made him conscious of his ignorance, he seeks to evade the problem by affirming
that everything is a matter of taste. In one sense this is true, but not in
the sense in which he means it. Every great artist has a personal bias.
It is this bias that constitutes his individuality, and we are justified

---

* *This chapter originally appeared as Chapter XIII of* Old Worlds for New: a Study of
the Post-Industrial State *(London: George Allen & Unwin, Ltd., 1917), pp. 110–116.*

in respecting such differences as arise from the individuality of great artists. These, however, are fundamentally different from the differences which arise from the idle fancies of undisciplined tastes, for the great artist submits his taste to a stern discipline. His spontaneity is the flower of that discipline, and it is just in proportion as a man can submit himself to this discipline that he takes his rank as an artist. I cannot insist too strongly upon the need of recognizing this truth. It is fundamental, and it will remain impossible to restore a tradition of art and handicraft until it is realized. The absence of any such tradition or common language of design is at the root of our difficulties today, for when everyone is, as it were, speaking a different language, artists have little chance of being understood. Now, a tradition bears the same relation to art as the command of language does to speech. Without a language it would be possible for a man to make noises, but words are necessary to enable him to express himself, and he must possess a good vocabulary if he wishes to convey his ideas and to make his meaning clear to others. So in respect to a tradition of art; without it, it is simply impossible for any man to design or express himself intelligently. The only way to recover such a medium of expression for the use of all is by the exercise of a rigid discipline in matters of taste.

When we realize how utterly false is the popular idea of art today, it is not surprising that it is neglected. Truth to tell, insofar as the art of today does approximate to the popular notion there is no purpose in supporting it. The sooner it dies a natural death the better. But real art is a different matter. No nation neglects its claims without being made to suffer for it, and this not only in the hideousness and rawness of its external life, but in a decline of general intelligence and in the growth of economic difficulties. For all these things are related to each other in subtle ways, and the great thinkers of every age have recognized it. Could we see that terrible monster, modern European materialistic civilization in its true light, we should realize that it owes its existence in no small degree to our neglect of the arts and their sweetening and refining influence. The best proof I can bring of this is that art and our civilization are antipathetic, not merely in the material, but in the spiritual sense. It is impossible to produce beautiful things for people who think like the moderns do when they are determined to have their own way. In this respect, Socialists as a body are no better than other people. Indeed, I often incline to think they are worse; for their habit of relating every evil in society to the growth of the economic problem is apt to blind them to aspects of truth, the recognition of which is not only indispensable to the solution of the problems of art, but of the economic problem itself.

I said that the popular idea of art was that it is a veneer or decoration added to something which would otherwise be ugly. This fallacy ultimately accounts for the neglect of the Arts and Crafts, because it leads the public to suppose that beauty is necessarily expensive. That, of course, is true, insofar as it depends upon honest workmanship and the use of good material, but that is all the truth there is in it. A table may be in good or bad proportion, it may be a pleasing or offensive colour, but neither proportion nor colour has anything to do with the cost. In each case what makes the difference is whether the designer has an eye for these things. Many artistic products are cheap, as the peasant arts of all countries which have not been exploited by commercialism bear witness. But the public neglect them. With their fixed idea that art is something added, and therefore costly, they refuse to buy such things. They prefer shoddy made imitations of more expensive forms of design. The consequence is that beautiful things which are inexpensive tend to go off the market. This stupid attitude of mind makes it difficult for the artist to be perfectly straightforward in his dealings with the public. He never knows what to charge. In many cases, if he charges a fair price and the price is low, they refuse to buy, on the assumption that it is not good work. If, knowing this, he prices his work high, as likely as not they will say that they cannot afford it. In a word, the artist in his dealings with the public today not infrequently finds himself between the devil and the deep blue sea. The public become the prey of sharks of all kinds, because it is almost impossible for honest men to handle them. They have only themselves to blame. It is this kind of nonsense that defeated the Arts and Crafts movement in its original intention, and it is this kind of nonsense that the capitalist knows how to exploit. It is the secret of half of his power.

There is another reason for the neglect of the Arts and Crafts. It is a spiritual failure. It is one of the paradoxes of our age that the public do not appear to mind how much they spend upon things of a temporary nature, but they grudge every penny spent upon things of permanent value. The proprietor of a West-End gallery where works of handicraft are sold, told me recently that ladies who would not mind giving fifteen or twenty guineas for a hat which only lasts a few months and which probably only costs as many shillings to make, yet will consider an article of craftsmanship at a similar price, which represents real value in labour quite apart from its aesthetic qualities, as outside their reach. It is perfectly extraordinary, when you get behind the scenes, to witness the vagaries of the public or to account for their motives in expenditure. No matter how huge a person's income may be nowadays, he rarely thinks he can afford to buy anything of permanent value. The vast mass of people fritter away their incomes in all kinds of senseless extravagance. They know no limit to personal expenditure, and are mean and contemptible in every other direction. And this spirit is not only confined to the rich. It is spreading to every class of society, down to the lowest. Have we not heard what the factory girl spends on dress?

Ruskin spent most of his life in trying to convince people that political economy is a moral science. He went to the root of the problem when he said: "The vital question for individual and nation is not, How much do they make? But, To what purpose do they spend?" It is a fruitful idea, and it receives ample corroborative testimony from the writings of the Chinese philosopher, Ku Hung Ming.[21] He says:—

> The final distress of China and the economic sickness of the world today are not due to insufficiency of productive power, to want of manufactures and railways, but to ignoble and wasteful consumption. Ignoble and wasteful consumption in communities, as in nations, means the want of nobility of character in the community or nation to direct the power of industry of the people to noble purposes. When there is nobility of character in a community or nation, people will know how to spend their money for noble purposes. When people know how to spend their money for noble purposes, they will not care for the "what," but for the "how" – not for the bigness, grandeur, or showiness, but for the taste, for the beauty of their life's surroundings. When people in a nation or community have sufficient nobility of character to care only for the tastefulness and beauty of their life's surroundings, they will want little to satisfy them, and in that way they will not waste the power of industry of the people, such as in building big, ugly houses and making long, useless roads. When the power of industry of the people in a community or nation is nobly directed and not wasted, then the community or nation is truly rich, not in money or possession of big, ugly houses, but rich in the health of the body and the beauty of the soul of its people.... Ignoble and wasteful consumption not only wastes the power of industry of the people, but it makes a just distribution of the fruits of that industry difficult.

THE RETURN TO THE PAST
from *Post-Industrialism*

O
NE OF THE CONSEQUENCES of giving to spiritual values the
foremost place is that we inevitably put the past before the
present, because the great traditions of culture come from
the past. Hence it has been that all great movements of human origin
in history – good and bad – have had their beginning in a study of
the past. All the movements in the Middle Ages began with a desire
to recover the culture and art of the Pagan world. The activities of
the Schoolmen[22] and the lawyers had their origin in such an attempt.
Gothic[23] architecture likewise had its origin in an attempt to revive
the old Roman architecture, the ruins of which covered the Empire.
The Renaissance[24] merely continued the same tradition of looking
back. But what made the Renaissance so deadly was not the fact that
it looked back, but the things that it looked back for. The Medieval
schoolmen looked back to recover lost truths to enable them to bring
light and understanding to men. But the men of the Renaissance
were prompted by a different motive. There were elements of pride
and egotism associated with their desire to revive antiquity. The
motive that inspired their passion for learning was not a communal
but an individualist one. It was not the salvation of society, but the
development of the individual. It was less the substance of Pagan
thought than the language or style, the way a thing was said, that
interested them. It was a movement of externals, and so it degenerated into pedantry. It became destructive. But this failure does not
prove the futility of revivals. What it does prove is the insufficiency
of the motives that prompted the men of the Renaissance. It will at
all times be necessary to look back if we are anxious to see life in its

---

* *This chapter originally appeared as Chapter VIII of* Post-Industrialism *(London: George Allen & Unwin, Ltd., 1922), pp. 137–157.*

proper perspective, for in the development of civilization the basic and fundamental things have a way of getting overlaid, obscured and forgotten, and it is only by searching in history that they may be recovered.

Fortunately in our day the truth of this principle – that the future may only be discovered in the past – has been strikingly demonstrated by the success that has attended the Sinn Fein movement in Ireland. To the average Englishman, Sinn Fein[25] is nothing more than a rebellion, like the Fenian rebellion against the overlordship of England. Yet it is only necessary to have a slight acquaintance with the movement to know it is more than this, since if such had been the case it would in all probability have ended in much the same way, degenerating into a secret physical force movement ending in another Fenian fiasco. If Ireland was saved from repeating this experience, it was because Sinn Fein dug deep down into the depths of human nature, because along with its political and revolutionary activities, it maintained other overt activities that kept the people together. The foundations of the movement were laid by the Gaelic League[26] which, established in 1893, came with intellectual illumination to safeguard the practical progress that was being made towards putting the Irish farmer on his feet by the Irish Agricultural Organization Society, the Congested Districts Board and the Department of Agriculture from degenerating into materialism. Its activities were consequent upon the labours of Dr. Douglas Hyde.[27] "If," says Mr. de Blacam,[28]

> Ireland today is not the Ireland of Carleton, Lover and Lever – the stage Ireland of drunkenness and brawling, ignorance and snobbery – but the Ireland of the Gaelic tradition, heroic, imaginative, daring – Dr. Hyde's scholarly labours are the source of the change. His *Literary History of Ireland*, a gigantic, ill-proportioned book overflowing, gossiping, absorbing volume, suggesting the rapid talk of an enthusiast, bubbling over with more news than he can tell of great discoveries – this was the book that revealed a wealth of cultural possessions that nine hundred and ninety-nine Irishmen were as ignorant of as they were of the writings of Krasinski[29] and Mickiewicz.[30] It threw a new light on Irish history, under which the figures and places of the past seem to take on a bright and splendid life. His pen was like a wand that

turned Ireland from a hovel to palace a of faëry grandeur in her sons' eyes. The Gaelic tongue, subtle, musical, elabourate, yet regarded with a slave's shame since Dan O'Connell[31] decried it, became now a fountain of intellectual life; and Anglo-Irish literature, catching the reflected light of Gaelic inspiration, shone with the name of Yeats,[32] Synge,[33] Gregory,[34] Colum O'Grady,[35] Russell,[36] Milligan[37].... A national drama rose; and Dublin, putting off its down-at-heels gentility, became an artistic centre, and an absorbingly interesting place to live in. So vigorous was the new cultural movement that men of the aristocrat caste or Protestant creed, men who formerly regarded Ireland as a place best out of, men who in early years became Bernard Shaws, now found in Ireland their most appreciative audience.

The early passion of the Gaelic revival was almost apostolic, religious, accompanied by signs and wonders, and none of us will ever forget his first *Feis,* marching through the green hills to the skirl of the pipes, or singing the memory-haunted Gaelic songs at the mossy shrines of heroes. Though it was scarce suspected then, we can now all see implicit in those early functions the developments that have since come to pass, and Sinn Fein, Republicanism and Social Gaelicism were inevitable out-flowerings of the seed then sown. All we knew then was that our feet were upon a mounting road with something splendid, though still cloud-shrouded, as the goal.†

So writes Mr. de Blacam of the literary movement that preceded the organization of Sinn Fein, "The uprise of a fine rural economy, accompanied by the growth of a literary production and an impassioned recourse to rich, forgotten fields of cultural inspiration, could not fail to issue in some energetic political movement, particularly when the existing political order was so repugnant to the new ideals."‡ Hence, in due course, there came the Sinn Fein policy of political abstention which owed its origin to Mr. Arthur Griffiths,[38] who in 1902 described in the *United Irishman* the tactics of abstention from the Austrian Parliament, which preceded Francis Joseph's[39] recognition of Hungarian independence under the Dual Crown,

---

† *What Sinn Fein Stands For,* by A. de Blacam (Chapman & Dodd), pp. 42–43.
‡ *Ibid.,* p. 44.

urging the adoption of the same policy. Instead of going to Westminster, let the Irish members form a National Council in Dublin and let the people obey its measures voluntarily. A State would thus be built up in opposition to the intruding State. The Imperial Parliament would find its machinery unworkable and would be obliged to recognize the *de facto* State created by the nation's self-determination. At a later date there came P. H. Pearse,[40] who gave the spark necessary to fire the train that Arthur Griffiths had laid. He taught a gospel of blood and sacrifice which transformed Sinn Fein into a militant party. To these names should be added that of James Connolly,[41] who in the 'nineties founded the Irish Socialist Republican Party, which gave to the movement a Socialist bias which eventually turned in the direction of a revival of Medieval economic teaching as being more in accord with the actual circumstances to be met.†

Now is there anything that we can learn from this experience of the Sinn Fein movement? I think there is. It should in the first place teach us that political and economic activity, pursued apart from a new ideal of life as expressed in spiritual values, is for the most part a vain delusion; inasmuch as apart from such values which give meaning to our activities, politics tends to lose touch with reality and degenerate into mere political opportunism, or into a secret, physical force movement. Next, it should teach us that if a movement is to grow in strength, it must not be based upon a nebulous anticipation of the future, but upon an effort to recover a forgotten and neglected past. For it is a paradox, but nevertheless true, that we can only go forward to a Golden Age in the future on the assumption that we appeal to a Golden Age in the past. The future is featureless, and to make it therefore the final court of appeal is to deny experience and to place ourselves inevitably at the mercy of every charlatan who comes along. For there can be no way of exposing the fallacies involved in a new heresy, except by some reference to some standard or experience of the past. The charlatan, therefore, in appealing to the future while denying the past discounts beforehand any possible criticism of his position, and cajoles the public into acquiescing in things which as often as not they know to be wrong. Failure to perceive the truth of

---

† *What Sinn Fein Stands For*, pp. 44–66.

these principles is at the root of the futility of Socialist and Labour politics, for it divorces them from all reality, leading them to suppose that there is such a thing as solving the social problem entirely in the terms of economics – unmindful of the fact that the economic evils of our society are finally nothing more than the obtrusive symptoms of an inward spiritual disease that has followed the separation of man from religion, art and nature, and which has changed the substance of our lives and activities.

But it will be said, granted that the principles followed by Sinn Fein are true, we cannot follow their example. This movement was possible in Ireland because the literary past of Ireland was a forgotten past, while such a revival provided something that could be posited against the dominance of English politics and culture, and therefore could be used to give the Irish people a belief in their own culture and destiny. But our circumstances are different. We have no forgotten literary past, nor do we suffer from a foreign yoke. How then can we proceed along Sinn Fein lines? In the literal sense, of course, we cannot. Yet though we proceed along different lines, we may acknowledge the same principles. If it is not open to us to revive a forgotten literary past, it is open to us to revive our own historic past; our social and industrial past, when there was a peasantry on the soil and craftsmen in the workshop, when things produced were beautiful and when, organized in Guilds, men lived a corporate life, when, in short, England was truly Merrie England. This past could be revived, and if it could not be posited against a foreign enemy, it could be posited against the enemy within our gates, against that industrial progress "whose motive is money and whose method is machinery."

The foundations of such a revival have already been laid by our various reform activities, and it needs but a frank acceptance of the principle of reversion to unite together in one revolutionary current for a common purpose activities which, pursued separately and without such a common objective, accomplish nothing. Hitherto what has stood in the way of such desideratum has been the popular belief that industrialism was a thing of permanence and stability, but nowadays when it is becoming widely recognized that this belief is a delusion, a path should before long be open to us; for when men can no longer look forward with equanimity, they will inevitably come to look back. When this change-over is a *fait accompli,* activities which the modern world has regarded as anachronisms will wear a different aspect. The activities of our agricultural organizations, societies and movements to restore the crafts and arts will appear full of significance as intelligent anticipations of the future.

With the agricultural aspect of this question, I do not propose to deal, as I have dealt with it elsewhere,† but will pass onto a consideration of the Arts and Crafts movement, which more than any other movement of our day is anti-industrial. Its activities were consequent upon the teachings of Ruskin and the experiments of William Morris in the revival of handicraft. Immediately, its aim was to unite the artist and craftsman, who under our mechanical system of production have become fatally divided to the detriment alike of art and craft. But the movement could not stop there; for the idea had social and economic implications. It became inevitably anti-industrial; for it is apparent that if social evolution, as we call it, had separated the artist and craftsman, further progress along present lines could only separate them still further. Hence the effort to unite the artist and craftsman involves the challenge of industrialism. This fact was frankly recognized by the leading members of the movement. Thus, writing on the aims of the movement, the late Mr. Walter Crane[42] said,

> The movement indeed represents, in some sense, a revolt against the hard mechanical life and insensibility to beauty (quite another thing to ornament). It is a protest against that so-called industrial progress which produces shoddy wares, the cheapness of which is paid for by the lives of their producers and the degradation of their users. It is a protest against turning men into machines, against artificial distinctions in art, and against making the immediate market value, or possibility of profit, the chief test of artistic merit. It also advances the claim of all and each to the common possession of beauty in things common and familiar, and would awaken the sense of this beauty, deadened and depressed as it now too often is, either on the one hand by luxurious superfluities, or on the

† *Guilds, Trade and Agriculture* (Allen & Unwin).

other by the absence of the commonest necessities and the gnawing anxiety for the means of livelihood; not to speak of the everyday ugliness to which we have accustomed our eyes, confused by the flood of false taste or darkened by the hurried life of modern towns in which huge aggregates of humanity exist, equally removed from both art and nature, and their kindly and refining influences.

It asserts, moreover, the value of the practice of handicraft as a good training for the faculties, and as our most valuable counteraction to that over-straining of purely mental effort under the fierce competitive conditions of the day; apart from the very wholesome and real pleasure in the fashioning of a thing with claims to art and beauty, the struggle with and triumph over technical necessities which refuse to be gainsaid. And, finally, thus claiming for man this primitive and common delight in things made beautiful, it makes, through art, the great socializer for a common and kindred life, for sympathetic and healthy fellowship, and demands conditions under which your artist and craftsman shall be free.

"See how great a matter a little fire kindleth." Some may think this is an extensive programme – a remote ideal for a purely artistic movement to touch. Yet if the revival of art and handicraft is not a mere theatrical and imitative impulse; if it is not merely to gratify a passing whim of fashion, or demand of commerce; if it has reality and roots of its own; if it is not merely a little colour at the end of a sombre day – it can hardly mean less than what I have written. It must mean either the sunset or the dawn.†

It seems a long way from this early war-cry to the Arts and Crafts movement of today. Yet it is not so far as it looks, for the Guild movement had its origin in the economic failure of the arts and crafts. Do not let us forget that the Guild movement was in the first instance floated upon the Arts and Crafts movement, and that in its early days the revival of handicraft was an integral part of the movement. But when the Guild idea spread outside of the sphere of the arts and crafts and was adopted by Socialists, this aspect of the movement was dropped, not being considered by National Guildsmen as a vital

---

† *Arts and Crafts Essays.* A collection of essays by members of the arts and crafts society. "The Revival of Handicraft," by Walter Crane.

issue. That from the point of view of propaganda, on the principle of one thing at a time, there was something to be said for separating the sociological from the craft ideas of the movement is not to be denied; for the principle of the Guild has applicability outside of the sphere of craftsmanship. But that the change has not all been gain is equally demonstrable; for in abandoning the revival of handicraft as a remote and inconsequential issue, the movement lost that grip on reality that it formerly possessed. It lost sight of the problems of machinery and the subdivision of labour which, as I have endeavoured to show, is the central economic issue; and as a consequence it no longer challenges Industrialism, which is the enemy, but only the financial aspect of it, which we designate as capitalism. So it has come about that while the movement has met with widespread success, we must recognize that it is after all only one of those half-successes that leads to ultimate impotence, as the present position of the National Guild movement bears witness.

Under these circumstances, it becomes apparent that the time has now come to reassert the more fundamental principles that were formerly associated with the Guild movement. Recognizing that the central problems of our age are those of machinery and the subdivision of labour, we must demand on the one hand that the use of machinery be regulated and the subdivision of labour abolished, and on the other hand we must set to work to rebuild what they have destroyed or are destroying. Foremost among these is the revival of handicraft, for to revive handicraft is to challenge all forms of mechanical production. And in this endeavour, circumstances should come to our aid; since as the days of industrial expansion are over and unemployment and short time have become the order of the day, it ought to be possible to secure popular support for the movement which has been impossible hitherto. Why should not those who are unemployed be trained in agriculture, and those on short time in handicrafts? Thus there might be brought into existence a new economic system within the existing industrial system in the same way that Sinn Fein brought into existence a State within a State.

But, it will be said, if such a policy is practicable, why should the Arts and Crafts movement have failed in its larger aims? The answer is because the Arts and Crafts movement was never organized except for exhibition purposes. It was a movement of pioneers, whose primary aim was to recover the traditions of design and handicraft. As such it was individualistic. The individual craftsman was left to fend for himself as best he could, and this was no easy matter because he generally found it impossible to borrow capital because craftsmanship was not considered good security, while he had to organize his own market because for a variety of reasons he could not avail himself of the ordinary channels of distribution. Unless, therefore, he were a many-sided person, very fortunately placed, with good social connections, had money, or could get friends to back him, he had little or no chance of success; for experience has proved that exhibitions are rarely followed by sales. Further, these difficulties are responsible for side-tracking the movement, for the more utilitarian a craft is, the larger must be the capital in these days. Hence it has been that, left to their own resources, the craftsmen were for the most part unable to concentrate on the utilitarian crafts which required large capital, and specialized in the decorative ones where little was required, and hence it has come about that the Arts and Crafts movement from being, among other things, a protest against the dependence of art on luxury, has become one of its feeders.

Such being the case, it is evident that a widespread revival of handicraft will not follow any mere extension of activities on the lines of the Arts and Crafts movement. On the contrary, the first thing to do is to create a popular belief in the ideals of craftsmanship by means of propaganda. Following that, there must be organization of the market and the provision of credits for craftsmen, who should be under the discipline of a Guild. If this were undertaken on a large scale as part of a national movement that sought to establish Guilds, fix prices, regulate machinery, and abolish the subdivision of labour, then it would be a practical proposition, but as an isolated issue attempted on a small scale it is beset with difficulties because in these days the market cannot be localized.

Though the Arts and Crafts movement failed in its wider aim, I think it can be claimed that it succeeded in restoring the traditions of handicraft and design in the sense that it brought into existence a number of craftsmen who knew what they were about, and has thus paved the way for the revival of craftsmanship on a larger scale, since the experimental work has now been done. There is no greater illusion than that harboured by modernists that the emancipation of the people from economic servitude would be followed by a spontaneous democratic revival of the arts, for that is not the way things come about. On the contrary, not only the history of art in the past but the progress that has been in the direction of its revival at the present day demonstrate beyond possibility of doubt that any awakening proceeds from the few to many, by the gradual widening of the circle of those who know what they are about. And the recognition of this principle is not incompatible with an equal recognition of the principle that the art of the future shall be a democratic art. For when we speak of a democratic art, of an art that shall be the common possession of the whole people, we do not mean that we expect that in some mysterious way art will spontaneously arise up among the people when they are liberated from economic servitude, but that we are anxious to promote a particular kind of art in which the people may eventually share, and it is because Medieval art† was in this sense democratic that we believe that it must form the basis of any revival of art in the future. Greek, Roman and Renaissance art, on the contrary, are autocratic and servile. This is necessarily the case because they are based upon conceptions of abstract form; and abstract form is just as incapable of forming a basis for popular art, as logic would be capable of forming a basis for a popular literature. Hence, when such an ideal of art is exalted, the mass of workers inevitably work under the dictation of a few. But with Medieval art it was different. In it there was a place for all. The master of abstract form found scope for his talents in the more generalized conceptions of Medieval art. But there was also a place for the individual craftsman, who was permitted to exercise his imagination on the details. That is what we mean by a democratic art, an art in which everyone would find a place and could share, not an art that is to be created by Tom, Dick and Harry, who have never given a moment's thought to the subject as some people suppose.

---

† By Medieval art I must be understood to refer not only to Romanesque, Byzantine, and Gothic art, but to the vernacular architecture and craftsmanship of the Renaissance in which the Medieval spirit survives – in a word, to all European art that rests on a basis of experimental handicraft.

I said that any widespread revival of art will follow the gradual widening of the circle of those who know what they are about. Any widening of this circle depends upon two things:— the removal of economic obstacles, and the cultivation of a certain temper or receptive attitude of mind on the part of the mass of people. It is with the second only of these that we are immediately concerned, for the difficulty which at the moment restricts such influences within comparatively narrow limits is the attitude which the majority of people adopt towards anybody who happens to know more than they do. People are apt to be very sensitive on matters of taste, especially if they have just a little of it, for a little taste, like a little knowledge, is a dangerous thing. It so often leads them to resent criticism. They resent the dogmatism of the artist as something which, if not resisted, would crush them. Yet this is not the case, for if they only knew it, submission would liberate the creative impulse within them. To learn in the arts as in other subjects depends on a certain humility of temper which will allow a man to subordinate himself to anyone whom he feels knows more about the thing than he does himself. If a man is willing to do this for a period, a time comes when he grows out of his pupilage and begins to feel his own feet. But there are very few who will do this. Their pride seems to stand in the way. Yet everything depends upon the cultivation of such a temper. Well did the Medieval Church rank pride as chief of deadly sins. It is the most deadly because it prevents a man from learning, compelling him to live on himself.

While, therefore, we may recognize that the solution of the economic problem is a precedent condition of the triumph of art in the world, let us not lose sight of the fact that a more immediate enemy is personal pettiness, since even under existing economic conditions there is no reason, apart from this personal pettiness, why things should be anything like as bad as they are. Hence the cultivation of a different temper to the prevailing one is a precedent condition of any widespread revival; for with any revival of art there must go a certain respect for mastership – a capacity for subordinating oneself to a master – while it is frustrated by the prevailing temper of self-assertion, both among artists whose pride leads them to desire to be thought original,† and the man-in-the-street who "knows what he

---

† The fact must not be lost sight of that this individualist and anarchist develop-

likes" and is unwilling to learn. The truth is that all great masters have been willing learners, and their dogmatism does not arise from pride or egotism, but from the self-confidence that follows patient study – the sure knowledge that they understand certain things and their anxiety to share it with others. The great artist always begins by subordinating himself to the needs of a communal tradition, and he ends by transcending it. The minor artist will not do this. He will not submit himself to such a discipline. He is so anxious to preserve his own individuality that he fails to achieve distinction in anything, coming finally to suffer from that most dreadful of human infirmities – that combination of small conceit and minor achievement which is associated with the "artistic temperament."

I said that a great artist subordinates himself to the needs of a great tradition. As such his spirit is democratic, for the true democratic spirit is not the one which merely seeks to give the public what they want, like the Northcliffe Press,[43] but one that can subordinate itself to what the public needs. Two very different things; for the time-server is the first; the great teacher is the second. In the world today, however, there is no established communal tradition of art. To what then does the great artist subordinate himself? The answer is to the communal traditions of the past. He chooses from among those great traditions a vehicle of expression, seeking always to transcend it. There is a great deal of nonsense talked among modernists about revivals who, in their anxiety to empty life of its last remaining contents, deprecate any study of the past as something that militates against the discovery of the future. But the truth is that it is impossible to discover the future apart from an understanding of the past, as the fact that modernists are invariably taken by surprise bears witness.

Immediately the Arts and Crafts movement sought to revive traditions of handicraft by re-uniting the artist and the craftsman; by implication it was anti-industrial, ultimately it was Medieval, for it was part of that wider Medieval Movement which, throughout the nineteenth century, sought to reverse the decision of the Renaissance

---

ment in art has economic as well as personal roots. To become successful the artist must in these days attract attention, which fact militates against the growth of a consecutive tradition of art, by encouraging stunts. For this evil there is finally no remedy apart from a more intelligent patronage which would remove the economic cause of this development.

in so many branches of activity. Many influences combined at the beginning of the last century to turn men's minds in the direction of the Middle Ages. There was, in the first place, a growing recognition of the fact that the influence of the Renaissance and the Reformation had been to empty life of its contents. Religion had become dry and superficial, learning had become pedantic, art a dilettante pose, architecture a lifeless formula, while politically and economically society found itself in the throes of convulsion. The French Revolution, upon which so many hopes were founded, had ended in disappointment, while the Industrial Revolution was "grinding the faces of the poor." The result of it all was that the need was widely felt for a deeper philosophy than current ideas afforded, and that need was not altogether unconnected with the literary influence of Sir Walter Scott,[44] who struck the first telling blow for Medievalism. Within the course of half a century Scottish life had undergone as complete a transformation as England had done in several hundred years; the destruction of the power of the Highland chiefs after the insurrection of 1745 having been followed by a rapid growth of commercial conditions of life and society. Scott had witnessed this sunset of Medievalism in his country and he sought to preserve in prose and verse some memory of a life that was disappearing around him. Of his influence on his age, Newman[45] says in the *Apologia*, "The general need of something deeper and more attractive than what had offered itself elsewhere, may be considered to have led to his popularity; and by means of his popularity, he reacted on his readers, stimulating their mental thirst, feeding their hopes, setting before them visions, which, when once seen, are not easily forgotten, and silently indoctrinating them with nobler ideas, which might afterwards be appealed to as first principles."

Contemporary with Scott were Coleridge,[46] Southey,[47] and Wordsworth,[48] who each in their own way carried their readers forward in the same direction. Their initial impulse came from disappointment with the course of the French Revolution and their hatred of industrialism and the pseudo-classicism of the eighteenth century. The leading spirit of this group was Coleridge, who visiting Germany had come under the influence of the Romantic Movement there. Though he has left no book which gives an adequate summary of his teachings, which for the most part consisted of religio-philosophical aphorisms, yet his personal influence was enormous. He was the most brilliant conversationalist of his age; and after about 1820 – the same date, it is interesting to observe, when Owen's[49] communist schemes and anti-capitalist economics began to find adherents – the young generation began to turn to him for guidance. Newman, Disraeli,[50] Morris, Kingsley,[51] and Ruskin among others were all either directly or indirectly influenced by him. The impulse thus given exercised a powerful influence on the thought of the age. Leading men's minds back to pre-individualistic times, when society was organized in corporate bodies with special responsibilities towards their members, it eventually crystallized itself into three movements – the Oxford Movement[52] in the Church of England, the Pre-Raphaelite movement[53] in painting, and the Gothic Revival[54] in architecture. These three movements, though differing in their primary aims and differing still more in their individual exponents, were nevertheless closely interwoven. They had one thing in common. The eyes of all were turned back on the Middle Ages as a common source of inspiration. To these movements are to be added the Arts and Crafts movement and the Guild movement, for though beginning in our day they continue the same tradition.

It is important that this page of history should be known. For in directing this our attack upon machinery and the subdivision of labour we are conscious not only of the fact that we are challenging the last defences of the existing system, but that we are carrying to its logical conclusion a tradition of thought and activity with a century of history behind it. It is thus we are strengthened by the knowledge that we are part of a great tradition – a tradition from which whatever is vital and healthy in the thought and life of today derives. For it has in turn exercised a rejuvenating influence upon religion, art and economics; and if after a century of effort these activities today falter, it is not because those who preceded us were mistaken in their aims, but that the time had not arrived when the citadel of the enemy could be successfully attacked. Before that was possible much spade work had to be done. The surrounding forts had one by one to be reduced. Nowadays this work has been done and there remains for us but one thing left to do – to concentrate our attack upon the subdivision of labour and the unrestricted use of machinery which are carrying our civilization to destruction.

THE CHURCH AND THE COMMON MIND
from *Towards a Christian Sociology*

W E SAW THAT THE BASIS of a Christian sociology was to be found in the mutual dependence of the love of God and one's neighbour. But if ideas are to exercise a permanent influence on the world of affairs, it is essential for them to be embodied in institutions. Hence the Church, which Our Lord founded and left behind Him to continue the work He had begun. It was, as we saw, not to be regarded as an end in itself, such as it has come to be, but as an instrument for the establishment of the Kingdom of God.

But though Jesus meant that the Church was to be considered as a means rather than end, He did not mean that a time would ever come when the Kingdom would be established once and forever; because, as a matter of fact, in the sense of finality it never can be established. On the contrary, if it is to continue living, its life must be renewed daily; and it is for this reason that the Church as a visible and organised institution will always be necessary. It will always be necessary, moreover, because Christianity is the religion of the Incarnation. Spirit and form, soul and body, cannot by the essential principle of faith be divided. To bring about harmony between them, between the inner and the outer life, between truth and its visible expression, between religion and civilisation is the task to which Christianity is committed. And as there can be no finality in these things, the Church will always be necessary to effect renewal and adjustment.

From a sociological point of view, the first function of the Church is to maintain in society the acceptance of common standards of thoughts and morals. This is a necessary condition of any stable

---

* *This chapter originally appeared as Chapter VI of* Towards a Christian Sociology *(New York: The MacMillan Company, 1923), pp. 47–54.*

social order, because if men are to share a common life they must share a common mind, for there must be a common mind if men are to act together. We have moved so far away from the thought and impulse of the Middle Ages that there are few today who recognise the fundamental importance of the common mind to any successful ordering of our social arrangements. Yet it is only necessary to reflect on the general social and political situation today to realise that in recognising its importance the Medievalists were right, while the Modernists in failing to do so are wrong. What is the secret of the apathy of the present day? The immediate cause is, doubtless, disillusionment. For centuries society has worshipped at the shrine of mammon, science, and mechanism. Men saw the immediate advantages which followed their surrender to them, while they concealed from themselves their evil side, which was tolerated, nay, justified, as incidental to the cause of progress. They refused to judge this development by any fixed standard of right and wrong, preferring to take their stand on the doctrine of evolution according to which any evil can be justified as a temporary phenomenon inevitable to a time of transition on the assumption that truth and justice will prevail in the end. But it has not worked out as expected. Experience has proved that figs do not grow on thistles, though the culture may be scientific. The pursuit of wealth has not resulted in a more equitable distribution, as Adam Smith[55] had prophesised, but has widened the gulf between rich and poor, while it is seen to end in widespread unemployment. It has corrupted business and politics, concentrated power, and built up irresponsible and impersonal tyrannies. Our industrial system has not liberated but enslaved men, while it uses up raw materials at such an alarming rate that the problem of securing new supplies has become a perpetual menace to peace. It is for such reasons that the feeling grows that modern civilisation is breaking up, while science, as detached as ever, invents poison-gas to ensure that the destruction shall be complete.

It is easy to understand why the awakening of the world to these perils should have led to some disillusionment. But the disillusionment would not have led to apathy but for another thing. The man of today has no idea how to stop the rot that threatens civilisation; and he has no idea how to stop it because there is no longer in existence a common mind; and because the common mind no longer exists it is impossible to secure any widespread agreement as to what requires to be done. For so long have men enjoyed freedom of thought and speech, for so long has such freedom been exalted as an end in itself, for so long has every false prophet who attacked the very foundations of right thinking and feeling enjoyed immunity, that the average mind today is in such a hopeless state of confusion about everything that it is impossible to get agreement about anything that really matters. And so it comes about that in the absence of any positive idea on which to unite, men today associate for negative purposes – not to promote what is right, but to denounce what is wrong; for after all, Socialist schemes of reconstruction are little more than organised negations, as the Labour Party's election manifesto bears witness. The desperate position in which, owing to the disappearance of a common mind, men find themselves today makes them attempt to co-operate by sinking their differences, on the assumption that the attainment of power is the first thing necessary to social salvation. But all such attempts avail nothing; for a power that is built up by sinking differences is not a real power but a sham one, that goes to pieces wherever it comes into collision with realities. It is for this reason that the Labour Party tends to lose effective strength in proportion as it grows in numbers. Its recent accession of strength† enables its voice to be heard, and will doubtless result in many things being done to mitigate existing evils that would not be done but for the fear of a Labour Government. To this extent, the Party is doing useful work. Yet the voice it raises is finally the voice of protest and negation rather than of a prophetic and constructive vision. The members of the Party can unite in their protests against war, on behalf of the unemployed, to prevent the decontrol of rents and in their attacks upon capital. But their points of agreement are superficial, while their disagreements are fundamental, and so it is an open question as to how long they will be able to remain united; for having put their trust in numbers rather than in clear thinking, their faith has become an amorphous conglomeration of conflicting beliefs, and it needs but the shock of reality to expose its weakness.

In these circumstances not only do we see the urgency of re-creating the common mind, but we begin to understand why in

---

† The General Election, November 15, 1922.

former times heresy was suppressed. It was suppressed because when men had a firm grip of fundamental truth they realised that any idea which attacked the unity of the Faith threatened the existence of the common mind, and therefore the stability of society by undermining its capacity to resist evil influences. It is for this reason that in the Middle Ages the heretic was looked upon as a traitor to society, and why for centuries the suppression of heresy was a popular movement. We miss the significance of this suppression if we assume that it was undertaken solely for ecclesiastical reasons. On the contrary, it is to be observed that the suppression of heresy has, with exceptions, been undertaken from secular rather than religious motives, and by civil rather ecclesiastical authorities, while there is nothing peculiarly Christian or Medieval about it. The Greeks condemned Socrates[56] to death because it was held that his teaching undermined respect for the gods, while Plato[57] finally came to the conclusion that to doubt the gods should be a crime punishable by death. The Roman Emperors persecuted the Christians for refusing observance of the gods, while it was the best Emperors who were opposed to the advance of Christianity and the worst ones who were indifferent to its encroachment – Marcus Aurelius[58] himself being no exception to this rule. And what is more interesting, it was not until Christianity became the official religion of the Empire that there was any persecution of heretics in the interests of Christianity. Then the successors of Constantine,[59] continuing in the persuasion of the Pagan Emperors that the first concern of the imperial authority was the protection of religion, persecuted men for not being Christians in the same spirit that their predecessors persecuted men because they were Christians. The same is true of the spirit in which heretics were persecuted by the Church. For it was not until the Papacy became a secular power that it began to persecute heretics, while the most active in their persecutions were the great Popes rather than the average ones, and all the great Popes, as Mr. McCabe[60] points out,† were canonists rather than theologians. Such persecutions, however, did not necessarily involve the death penalty, which was reserved for the very exceptional and obstinate cases; for, generally-speaking, the opinion prevailed among influential ecclesiastics that while the civil

† *Crises in the History of the Papacy,* by Joseph McCabe.

arm might be employed to deal with heretics by prohibiting assemblies and in other ways preventing them from spreading their views, the death penalty was contrary to the spirit of the Gospel. And this attitude continued until the close of the twelfth century when, owing to the spread of the heresy of the Albigensians[61] (which owing to the support of the nobility of Southern France, presented the aspect of a powerful political party in addition to that of an heretical sect), the attitude of the Church changed. The Church was terribly afraid of this new spirit, which She considered not only menaced her own existence but the very foundations of society as well, and in the end she shrank from no cruelty that she might be rid of it forever. The persecution of the Albigensians was the great crime of the Middle Ages, but it is interesting to observe that Innocent III,[62] who instigated the persecution, was a canonist rather than a theologian.

Sufficient has now been said to demonstrate that the suppression of heresy was undertaken for social rather than religious reasons; because men felt that the promotion of ideas which destroyed the unity of Faith was subversive of the social order. As to whether they were right in supposing that force was the remedy is quite another matter. But this much is certain: that men in the past were right in regarding the preservation of the common mind as a matter of supreme and fundamental importance to the stability of society; while it is equally certain that any solution of our difficulties at the present day involves its recovery; for if order is to be restored to the world, it will have to make its appearance first in the mind of man. And if order is to make its appearance in the mind of man, it will be because the world returns to Christianity. In the break-up of the modern world Christianity is the one thing that is left standing. Its principles are still vaguely accepted by an enormous mass of people today, and that is why it must become the new centre of order – a rallying point from which the traditions of society, of a common mind, can be re-created.

But it will be said: If we are to wait until the revival of Christianity is an accomplished fact, we are lost, for the problem confronting society develops with such rapidity, and we cannot expect any wholesale conversions of men to Christianity. To which I answer that I am speaking of the ultimate solution, not of immediate measures. But it would clarify our thinking enormously about practical measures if we considered them in the light of Christianity instead of in the light of the materialist philosophy. It is for this reason that the formulation and popularisation of a definitely Christian sociology which would relate the principles and forms of social organisation to the principles of Christianity is a matter of urgency. For in this our immediate task of re-creating the common mind, we cannot rely upon any purely educational propaganda which would aim directly at the creation of common standards of thought and morals; for such a propaganda would lack the definiteness necessary to the crystallization of thought. It is for this reason that there remains but one path of approach – to approach the spiritual through the material. We must meet the public half-way, bringing light to bear upon the problems in which they are interested, tackling the concrete realities of life and society. By such means the principles of Christianity would be brought into a close and definite relationship with the thought of today. And from the union would be born a common mind.

Notes.

[1] John Ruskin (1819–1900). Artist, scientist, poet, philosopher and art critic. He helped the Pre-Raphaelites to establish their reputation through his written interventions, and did much to support artists such as Rossetti, Millais and Holman Hunt. His major work, first published in 1871 as *Fors Clavigera*, was subtitled *Letters to the Workmen and Labourers of Great Britain*, and ran ultimately to eight volumes.

[2] Thomas Carlyle (1795–1881). Victorian writer and historian, whose *Collected Works* run to some 30 volumes and include *On History* (1830), *Sartor Resartus* (1833) and *On Heroes, Hero Worship and the Heroic in History* (1841). He was noted also for his emotional and intuitive approach to social questions, in contrast to that of the rationalist political economists.

[3] Matthew Arnold (1822–1888). Victorian-era poet and cultural critic. Graduate of Baliol College, Oxford. Wrote and published several volumes of poetry from roughly 1849 to 1855, after which time he devoted his efforts mainly to literary and cultural criticism, though with some notable exceptions (such as his 1867 volume, *New Poems*). In the first of many attempts to bring culture and criticism to the English middle class, he wrote *Culture and Anarchy* (1897–1869); therein he attacked (while coining the term) the "philistines." He once wrote to Cardinal Newman (*vide infra*), "There are four people, in especial, from whom I am conscious of having learnt...habits, methods, ruling ideas, which are constantly with me; and the four are – Goethe, Wordsworth, Sainte-Beuve, and yourself."

[4] William Morris (1834–1896). English artist, author, journalist and social activist. A leading Victorian era critic of Industrialism, he was an eclectic Socialist who was also variously influenced by the Oxford Movement as well as the legacy of medieval life and art. In 1856, he embarked on an artistic career, becoming famous for his poetry, wallpapers, designs, writings, and typography. He was the chief inspiration behind the Arts and Crafts movement (1870–1900) which desired to elevate the applied arts to the status of Fine Arts, and to restore a human dimension to the production of useful goods. His critique of industrialism led him to embrace Socialism; in 1884 he founded the Socialist League, and for a time was editor of its journal, *Commonweal*. He refused the Poet Laureateship in 1891, following Tennyson's death.

[5] Penty went to America – New York, specifically – sometime around May of 1906 to take a position with a large furniture firm, following limited success in designing furniture in London. He returned to England about the same time in 1907.

[6] Anglo-Catholic. The author is not here referring to the High-Church section of the Anglican Communion but rather to those Catholics and Anglicans in England who were both individually and collectively involved in the social critique of the times from a fundamentally Christian perspective.

[7] Lydia. An important commercial center in western Asia Minor. According to Herodotus, the Lydian kings were the first to strike coins in gold and silver.

[8] A chantry is an endowment for priests to sing the Holy Mass for the founder's soul. The 1547 Act was passed during the reign of King Edward VI (1547–1553), in the context of the Protestant Reformation. The act made the endowments and all associated chapels and religious institutions associated with them illegal, and thus effected their dissolution.

[9] Aristotle (384–322BC). Chief philosopher of the "realist" school and one of the wisest of all pagan philosophers; referred to simply as *"the* philosopher" by St. Thomas Aquinas, and by Maritain (in his *Introduction to Philosophy*) as the "philosopher *par excellence."* In 367BC, he went to Athens; there he studied under Plato for 20 years. Later he tutored Alexander the Great of Macedonia. Returning to Athens he founded his own academy for philosophy, the Lyceum, which became known as the "peripatetic school" because of his habit of teaching while walking. His most famous works include *Politics, Nichomachean Ethics,* and *Metaphysics.* Not only did Aristotle purify his teacher's doctrine of its errors; he bequeathed to philosophy itself a secure and commonsense foundation.

[10] St. Thomas Aquinas (1225–1274). The official Philosopher of the Catholic Church. His first Summa was the *Summa of Christian Teaching,* which was prepared specially to deal with those who did not have the Catholic faith: pagans, Jews, Greek schismatics and Muslims. His second, begun in 1266, was the *Summa Theologica* for which he is most famous, and which was a beginner's (!) introduction to Catholic theology. Mary Clarke, the Thomist writer, says: "To know St. Thomas is to know the medieval mind at its finest, its most powerful, and, indeed, its most modern. For he is timeless and timely, a man for all ages."

[11] Alfred Milnes (1849–1921). Free trade economist, lecturer, and statistician who also studied the vaccination question in England.

[12] Puritanism. A movement that began early in the reign of Queen Elizabeth I of England – circa 1560 – as a movement to "purify" (hence, "Puritan") the Church of England, which, it was maintained, was still too Catholic in hierarchy, vestment, and ritual. The Puritans were strong Calvinists, stressing Predestination and demanding *scriptural* warrant for every aspect of public worship. By the late 1560s, some of them had already adopted the Genevan ceremony of Calvin.

[13] Charles I (1600–1649). King of England from 1625 to 1649. Having inherited both the financial and religious problems of his country from his father, he sought to build up the Monarchy as a rallying point for all Englishmen beyond their confessional beliefs, so as to destroy the Parliamentary and financial cabal which sought his overthrow. His contest with Parliament and the Money Power resulted in Civil War and ended in his murder by Parliament in 1649. Hilaire Belloc's *Charles I* gives a stirring yet objective account of this intelligent man trapped in desperate national circumstances.

[14] A reference to the October, 1929, collapse of the financial markets in Wall Street which inaugurated the Great Depression, and which put a generation out of work throughout the West and destroyed countless families and businesses. It was only brought to an end when the re-armament process began, reaching "fruition" in WW II. Although "orthodox" historians and economists talk of the Crash as something "out of the blue," it was predicted years before by more astute observers. In *The Truth about the Slump* (1931), A.N. Field wrote: "No greater mistake can be made than to suppose that the present slump in commodity prices is due to blind economic forces. The depression from which we now suffer is due to an *artificially induced* variation in the purchasing power of money" (emphasis ours).

[15] Gustave le Bon (1841–1931). French psychologist and sociologist. Authored a number of works on social psychology in which he expounded his theories about

national traits and racial superiority. His best known works are: *The Crowd: A Study of the Popular Mind* (1897), *The Psychology of Socialism* (1899), and *The Psychology of Revolution* (1912).

[16] Ludditism. A reference to the beliefs of the Luddites, a loosely organized movement of opposition to factory machinery, which originated with the uprisings of workingmen in England, in areas such as Nottinghamshire, Lancashire, Cheshire, and Yorkshire, ca. 1811–1816. One of the first steps taken in the early phase of the Industrial Revolution was to replace English weavers' home looms with mechanized knitting and shearing machines, and power looms. The weavers, who saw in the machines a threat to their livelihoods, rioted and began to destroy the factory machines, acting in the name of the mythical "King Ludd" or "Ned Ludd," whose name would often be found inscribed on factory walls following a bout of destruction. The rioters thus became known as the "Luddites." Alternatively, Nicols Fox suggests in his *Against the Machine: The Hidden Luddite Tradition* (2002) that Ned Ludd was himself an abused weaving apprentice who took a hammer to the new machinery.

[17] Stuart Chase (1888–1985). Progressive economist, consumer activist, and author. He was the Director of the New York-based Labor Bureau which provided research, accounting, and other professional services to trade unions and co-operatives; it also published the *Facts for Workers* newsletter. In 1927 Chase founded Consumer's Research with Fred Schlink, with whom in the same year he produced an exposé of advertising and pricing practices used by capitalist manufacturers entitled *Your Money's Worth*. It was an instant success; by 1930 Consumer's Research had over 12,000 members. Chase also wrote on semantics, economic theory, and the history of technology, and was a regular contributor to journals such as *The Nation, The Forum,* and *The Outlook.*

[18] Richard Bartlett Gregg (1885–1974). American Quaker and pacifist political writer. A friend of Martin Luther King and an acknowledged expert on Gandhi and his movement; his works include: *The Power of Non-Violence* (1934), *Discipline for Non-Violence* (1941), *The Value of Voluntary Simplicity* (1936), *A Pacifist Programme* (1939), and *A Philosophy of Indian Economic Development* (1958).

[19] Dr. Lawrence Pearsall Jacks (1860–1955). British Unitarian minister, writer, interpreter of modern philosophy, and editor of the *Hibbert Journal* from its founding in 1902 to 1948. An early President of the Society for Psychical Research, who wrote the book *Near the Brink* (1952). In his book *My Neighbour the Universe: a Study of Human Labour* (1928), he says that in each piece of matter "the universe stands represented and speaks as a whole, saying to the worker: 'make me better.'"

[20] Penty is referring to German philosopher Friedrich Nietzsche (1844–1900).

[21] Ku Hung Ming (1857–1928). Chinese philosopher of the Qing dynasty who wrote deeply on the Chinese and the Chinese language, illustrating the spirit and value of the Chinese people. He believed that foreigners impaired the health of China.

[22] The Schoolmen. Catholic theologians who applied Scholasticism, both as a method and as a system, to Theology and Philosophy. Although the Golden Age of the Schoolmen was the thirteenth century, it is generally accepted that the Schools began their life in the ninth century. Amongst the many eminent thinkers of the Schools we find St. Bernard, St. Anselm, St. Thomas Aquinas, and St. Albert Magnus. Penty is referring to the fact that one of their chief achievements was to

present pagan philosophy (particularly Aristotelianism) to the Catholic world, and to make use of it to explain theological truth.

[23] The Gothic period in art history extends from roughly the fifth century to the sixteenth century, when the European Middle Ages came to an end. The art was of a fundamentally religious nature, and the period was distinctive for its arched design in churches, for its stained glass windows, and for its illuminated manuscripts. Important figures in this period were Master Guglielmo (12th-century Italian sculptor), Giottino (14th-century Italian painter), André Beauneveu (14th-century Dutch painter), and Henri Bellechose (15th-century Flemish painter).

[24] Renaissance. French for "rebirth," it refers to the radical and comprehensive changes that took place in Europe in the fifteenth and sixteenth centuries consequent upon the increasing interest of scholars, artists, and men of letters to re-discover the works of the pagan Greeks and Romans. The period represents the end of the medieval age and the beginning of the modern world; it is today regarded as a distinctive period in music, literature, and the arts.

[25] Sinn Fein. A radical Irish nationalist party founded in 1905 by Arthur Griffith (1871–1922) (*vide infra*) and Bulmer Hobson (1883–1969). Its founding brought together an eclectic mix of individuals and traditions; for a long time it had no real influence in practical politics – though its demand for Ireland to be an equal partner with England in a kind of Dual Monarchy, along with its thoughts on economic independence, had widespread effect on Irish political thinking. The movement was wholly radicalised in the wake of the 1916 Easter Rising in Dublin, although it took no part in the revolt. By 1918 it had recruited 112,000 members and had secured 73 of the 105 seats in Parliament. Following the establishment of the Irish Republic, it went into steep decline only to resurface in the 1960s in the context of the turbulent politics of the North of Ireland.

[26] The Gaelic League (*Connradh na Gaeilge*). An Irish language organization founded in 1893 by Eoin MacNeill and others, with Dr. Douglas Hyde (1860–1949) (*vide infra*) as first President. Unlike previous language groups, it sought to revive Irish as a spoken and literary language, and to that end Irish-speaking social events and language classes were organized. In 1897 it established a national festival, *An tOireachtas*, and a paper, *Claidheamh Soluis*. Although strictly non-political, it did much to promote Irish identity and pride in the Irish past. By 1914, it was largely taken over by the Irish Republican Brotherhood, with the result that many of the League's members played a prominent role in the 1916 Rising.

[27] Dr. Douglas Hyde (1860–1949). Irish Protestant academic and cultural revivalist. His first speech as President of the National Literary Society in 1892 was entitled, "The Necessity for De-Anglicizing the Irish People" – and it called for radical and immediate action. He was Professor of Irish History at University College, Dublin, from 1909 to 1932, and was the first President of Ireland from 1938 to 1945. He wrote extensively; his works included *The Love Songs of Connacht* (1893), *The Religious Songs of Connacht* (1906), and *A Literary History of Ireland* (1899).

[28] Aodh de Blacam (1890–1951). Irish Protestant journalist and convert to Catholicism. In 1915 he began writing extensively for Catholic and Republican journals, advocating a neo-Gaelic Irish Catholic society. He was a fervent supporter of Catholic Social Teaching, a trenchant critic of the evils of Capitalism, and an advo-

cate of the Corporative efforts of Franco and Salazar. Later in life he joined *Clann na Poblachta* because he was disappointed with the politics of Eamon de Valera's republican party, *Fianna Fáil*, especially its lack of concern for rural Ireland.

[29] Count Sigismund Krasinski (1812–1859). Strongly patriotic Polish poet of the Romantic literary movement. A prolific writer, his works include *The Infernal Comedy* (1833), *Iridium* (1836), *Psalms of Faith, Hope, and Love* (1845), and *Psalms of Sorrow and of Goodwill* (1848). Acclaimed as one of Poland's finest Catholic literary exponents, his work is notable for its emphasis upon the need for politics to be based upon Christian principles.

[30] Adam Mickiewicz (1798–1855). Advocate of Polish national freedom and leader of the Polish Romantic school; regarded as the country's finest poet. He spent time in prison for his beliefs, and was a friend of poet Alexander Pushkin (1799–1837). In 1848 he set up the "Mickiewicz Legion" to fight Austria; the same year he was granted an audience by Pope Pius IX. An advocate of radical social reforms, he used poems, lyrics, ballads, poetic tales, dramas, and novels to urge a Polish revival. His most famous works are *Forefathers Eve* (1832) and *Master Thaddeus* (1834).

[31] Daniel O'Connell (1775–1847). Irish political leader who first came to prominence in January 1800 when he was a part of the minority of Catholics who opposed the Act of Union with England. A capable lawyer, he possessed great oratorical and organizing abilities which he devoted to the cause of Catholic emancipation. As creator of the tactic of mass agitation in Ireland, he became a hero for 19th-century moderate nationalists. Dublin's famous O'Connell Street is named in his memory.

[32] William Butler Yeats (1865 – 1939). Poet and Irish Senator (1922–1928).

[33] John Millington Synge (1871–1909). A graduate of Trinity University in Dublin who lived for a time, at Yeats's suggestion, on the remote Aran Islands of Ireland, and which resulted in his *The Aran Islands* (1907). In time he became celebrated for his plays about Irish peasant life; his work *Riders to the Sea* (1905) is widely regarded as one of the finest tragedies ever written. It was produced at the Irish National Theatre – later the Abbey Theatre – in 1904. Others of his works include *The Well of the Saints* (1905), *The Playboy of the Western World* (1907), and *The Tinker's Wedding* (1908).

[34] Isabella Augusta Persse, the Lady Gregory (1852–1932). Figure of the Irish literary revival; wife of Sir W.H. Gregory. Through his extensive offices she met at their London home people like Browning, Tennyson, Millais, and Henry James. She visited Inisteer – one of the Aran Islands – in 1892 and thereafter learned Irish and the Hiberno-English dialect of Kiltartan. Along with Hyde and Yeats, she founded the Irish Literary Theatre in 1899. Writing extensively on all things Irish, she produced 19 plays as well. She is best remembered for her book *The Kiltartan History Book* (1909) and her work with Yeats on *Cathleen Ni Houlihan*.

[35] Probably a reference to Standish O'Grady (1846–1928), Irish historian and writer who played a leading role in the Irish literary revival. He wrote *The History of Ireland* (1878–1880) and produced many English language versions of the Irish heroic legends, including the celebrated *Cucuchlain* (1892–1917). He was also interested in the social question, and he contributed a series of articles to Jim Larkin's *Irish Worker* during 1912–1913, calling for the Dublin unemployed to be relocated to centres of Irish rural civilization where they could work in a decentralized economy given over to co-operative ownership and management.

[36] George Russell (1867–1935). Irish author who often wrote under the pseudonym "A. E." An active Irish nationalist; editor of the *Irish Homestead* from 1904 to 1923 and of the *Irish Statesman* from 1923 to 1930. He is regarded as one of the greatest writers of the Irish Literary revival.

[37] Alice Milligan (1865–1953). Active Irish nationalist, campaigner for the Irish language with the Gaelic League (*vide supra*), and writer. She was a co-founder of the Belfast publication *Northern Patriot,* and the editor of *Shan Van Vocht,* a Republican paper which carried, in 1897, the historically important work *Socialism and Nationalism,* by James Connolly.

[38] Arthur Griffith (1871–1922). Irish political leader and journalist. Founded the Celtic Literary Society in 1892; active in the Gaelic League (*vide supra*). He edited several radical papers, including *Sinn Fein* and *The United Irishman.* His elaboration of the need for Irish independence and for economic protectionism came to be accepted in the wider Irish nationalist movement. He founded Sinn Fein in November 1905 and, although he took no part in the 1916 Rising, he was made Head of the Plenipotentiaries who negotiated the Anglo-Irish Treaty of 1922. He was elected President of the Dáil in the same year.

[39] Franz Joseph I (1830–1916). Emperor of Austria and King of Hungary. The last significant Habsburg monarch who rose to the throne in 1848; was known for his simplicity of manners and accessibility even to the poorest of his subjects. Already in decline as a "great power," Austria under his reign lost Lombardy and Venetia. He created the Austro-Hungarian Dual Monarchy in 1867, but this did not halt the decline, and his wife was murdered by Italian anarchists in 1898. His nephew, Franz Ferdinand, was murdered in June 1914 by a member of the Serbian Masonic group "Black Hand," setting the stage for WW I.

[40] Patrick Pearse (1879–1916). Educationalist, writer, and Irish revolutionary. He began as a cultural nationalist, and edited the Gaelic League's journal, *Claidheamh Soluis,* from 1903 to 1909. In 1908 he founded St Enda's school, a bi-lingual secondary school that fostered all things Irish. He later joined the Irish Republican Brotherhood and was influential in building support for the 1916 Rising, in the wake of which he was shot by the British for having been the President of the Provisional Government declared at the outbreak of the Rising. He was a prolific writer who believed that bloodshed was less awful than slavery.

[41] James Connolly (1868–1916). Irish labor leader born in Edinburgh, Scotland. Imbibed his Irish nationalism from a Fenian uncle and his Socialism from the extremely grim life of the working class of the day. Became the head of the Irish Transport and General Workers Union, when Jim Larkin went to America following the collapse of the 1913 Lockout. A prolific writer, his best known works are *Labour in Irish History* (1910) and *The Re-conquest of Ireland* (1915). Became the military commander of the Easter Rebellion in 1916, and was executed sometime after. Despite his socialist convictions, he died in communion with the Church.

[42] Walter Crane (1845–1915). Apprentice at William Linton's engraving shop in London, leading to his fame for both his illustrative skills and his politics. While working with Linton, an ex-Chartist, his political views took shape, and he was variously exposed to the writings of Mill, Shelley, and Ruskin. Eventually he became a friend of William Morris and a sympathizer with Socialism. Detesting modern

manufacture and commercialism, he joined the Art Workers' Guild and the Arts and Crafts Society; he produced wallpapers, printed fabrics, tiles, and ceramics, and became Head of the Royal College of Art in 1898. His books include *The Claims of Decorative Art* (1892), *The Bases of Design* (1898), and *Line and Form* (1900).

[43] The Northcliffe Press. A reference to the papers owned by Alfred Harmsworth, Lord Northcliffe (1856–1922), who purchased his first newspaper, *The Evening News,* in 1894 and then went on to found the *Daily Mail* in 1896, which is still a major British tabloid. He was, and is, widely regarded as the man who began the dumbing-down of newspaper readerships, by including in his paper innovations such as sports pages, "human interest stories," a women's section, and the large banner headlines. He once said: "when I want a peerage I will buy one" – reinforcing the belief of many such as Chesterton and Belloc that peers were largely created *by* and *for* money. David Lloyd-George described Northcliffe as "one of the biggest intriguers and most unscrupulous people in the country."

[44] Sir Walter Scott (1771–1832). Scottish novelist and poet. Studied and practised law; his real interests were German literature and traditional ballads. His first publication was a translation of ballads by Gottfried Burger (1796) and later of Goethe's *Gotz von Berlichinegen* (1799). His first original work–though it and many others remained anonymous until 1827–was the successful *Lay of the Last Minstrel* (1805), followed by *Marmion* (1808), *The Lady of the Lake* (1810), and *Waverley* (1814). Others of his many works are *Rob Roy* (1818), *Ivanhoe* (1820) and *Red Gauntlet* (1824).

[45] Cardinal John Henry Newman (1801–1890). Philosopher, man of letters, and leader of the Oxford Movement in the Church of England. Converted to Catholicism in 1845 after completing his *Essay on the Development of Christian Doctrine;* was made a Cardinal in 1879. His most famous work – amidst a life full of writing and speaking – is his *Apologia pro Vita sua.* He was a life-long enemy of Liberalism.

[46] Samuel Taylor Coleridge (1772–1834). English poet, critic, writer, and speaker. With his friend William Wordsworth (1770–1850) he published *Lyrical Ballads* in 1798. In 1817 he published a critical text entitled *Biographia Literaria,* followed by a three-volume work, *The Friend* (1818). Amongst his best-known poems are *The Aeolian Harp, Christabele,* and *Kubla Khan.* On distinguishing Prose and Poetry, he wrote: "Prose...words in their best order. Poetry...the best words in the best order."

[47] Robert Southey (1774–1843). English poet, philosopher, and political radical. Became the co-editor of Lord Grenville's magazine, *The Flagellant,* in 1792. With Coleridge he shared a tempestuous friendship, a disgust with British political and educational policy, and authorship of two dramas, *The Fall of Robespierre* (1794) and *The Devil's Walk* (1799). He wrote *Wat Tyler* in 1794, based upon the Peasants' Revolt of 1381, which exposed his Republican tendencies; though the work did not appear until 1817, by which time he had changed his political views radically. He wrote his better-known works, *Joan of Arc, Thalaba the Defender,* and *Madoc,* between 1796 and 1805. Became Poet Laureate in 1813.

[48] William Wordsworth (1770–1850). English poet born into a comfortable family in Cumbria. Known as one of the "Lake Poets" because of the proximity of his house and work to the Lake District of the region. Said to be the most prolific poet ever, having penned over 70,000 lines of verse, focusing mainly upon Nature, children, and the common people. His important works appeared between 1797 and 1808,

and include *Lines Composed a Few Miles above Tintern Abbey, Poems* (in two volumes), and "I Wandered as Lonely as a Cloud." Became Poet Laureate in 1842.

[49] Robert Owen (1771–1858). Welsh Socialist and textile businessman. He bought the Chorton Twist Company in New Lanark, Scotland, in the 1790s; the company rapidly expanded. Not solely interested in profit, he attempted to create a new community around the factory. He believed that people would be good if they lived in a good environment, and to that end he built a school and a nursery for the 2,000 people of the village. He toured the country speaking about the New Lanark experiment but his words fell upon deaf ears. He moved to America in 1825 and set up a socialist community called New Harmony, but it too came to nothing. He sold his textile business in 1827 and through his two journals, *The Crisis* and *The New Model World,* he continued to preach factory reform, adult suffrage, and trade unionism. He wrote *The Formation of Character* (1813) and *A New View of Society* (1814).

[50] Benjamin Disraeli (1804–1881). British politician of Jewish descent who was variously a Conservative, a Whig, a Radical, and an Independent. Helped form the *Young England* group in 1842 which advocated an alliance between the working classes and the aristocracy; the doctrine appeared in his novels *Coningsby* (1844), *Sybil* (1845) and *Tancred* (1847). He became Prime Minster in 1868.

[51] Charles Kingsley (1819–1875). Anglican cleric and social reformer. Was greatly influenced by F. D. Maurice's work, *The Kingdom of Christ* (1838), which argued that politics and religion were inseparable and that the Church had to be involved in social questions. Following a period as a Chartist, Kingsley founded, with Maurice (1805–1872) and Thomas Hughes (1822–1896), the Christian Social Movement. Between 1848 and 1851, Kingsley contributed various articles to *The Politics of the People* and *The Christian Socialist* under the pseudonym "Parson Lot." He was Professor of History at Cambridge University (1860–1869) and wrote a number of works including *Alton Locke* (1850), *Hypatia* (1853), and *The Water Babies* (1863).

[52] Oxford Movement. A movement within the Church of England from 1833 to 1845 which attempted to emphasize the "continuity" of the Anglican Communion and the primitive Christian Church and thus with the Catholic Church. John Henry Newman (*vide supra*), whose conversion to Catholicism led many thousands of Anglicans to do likewise, was the driving force behind the movement, and he himself characterized it in hindsight as simply an attempt to draw Anglicans back into the Roman Church from which they had come out at the Reformation. The figures of the movement published various *Tracts for the Times,* becoming known therefore as Tractarians. Eventually, the movement broke down upon the impossibility of reconciling what Lord Chatham called (speaking of the Church of England) "a Popish liturgy, Calvinistic articles, and an Arminian clergy." Other leading lights – though not all arrived at Rome's door – included John Keble (1792–1865), J.A. Froude (1802–1836), E.B. Pusey (1800–1882), and J.B. Morris (1812–1880). The conversion of Cardinal Manning (1808–1892) in 1851 took place as a consequence of the work of the Tractarians and of Newman's *Development of Doctrine.*

[53] Pre-Raphaelites. A group of nineteenth century English painters, poets and critics who reacted against Victorian materialism and "neo-classical" artistic conventions. They were inspired by medieval and early Renaissance painters up to the time of Italian painter and architect Sanzio Raphael (1483–1520). The essentially Christian

movement was established in 1848 and included D.G and W.M. Rossetti, John Millais, James Collinson, John Ruskin (*vide supra*), and William Morris (*vide supra*).

[54] The Gothic Revival. A movement of architects, artists, and social critics, based on their appreciation of medieval principles and values such as craftsmanship, quality, and beauty, and designed to put those principles into practice in architecture, domestic decoration, and crafts. The first to popularise medieval values seriously in architecture was Augustus W. N. Pugin (1812–1852), who designed numerous churches in England on the gothic model. Ruskin (*vide supra*) was the leading social critic of the movement, and Morris (*vide supra*) its leading craftsman.

[55] Adam Smith (1723–1790). Scottish political economist and philosopher whose lasting fame is due to his major work, *The Wealth of Nations*, written in 1776. Was Professor of Moral Philosophy at Glasgow University (1752–63) and also wrote *The Theory of Moral Sentiments* (1759). A friend of the rationalist David Hume (1711–1776); in 1763 became tutor to the young duke of Buccleuch, an employment which was the motive for his lengthy visit to France (1764–1766). This visit brought him into contact with the famous "Encyclopedists," notables (noteworthy for their irreligion, skepticism, and rationalism) of the so-called French "enlightenment." These include D'Alembert (1717–1783), Helvétius (1715–1771), and particularly François Quesnay (1694–1774), the Physiocrat who, as one of the founders of economic liberalism, exercised such great influence over Smith's later writings. Celebrated Catholic economist C. S. Devas remarks of him, "[his] true position...is that of the great interpreter of the Physiocrats to the English world, and the great apostle in the British Isles of economic liberalism. His particular merit is that he is so much better than the doctrines he represented.... Thus, like all great men caught in erroneous systems, he is full of inconsistency" (*Political Economy*, 1891, p. 553).

[56] Socrates (469–399BC). Athenian philosopher who rescued Greek philosophy from the crass utilitarianism of the Sophists, and who focused it correctly upon the true nature of things by emphasizing man's obligation to the moral Good. He left no literary legacy, so that his life and works are known only through the writings of contemporary figures like Aristophanes and Xenophon, as well as Plato, his pupil. He was condemned to death for "interfering with religion" and "the corruption of youth" – a condemnation that he fulfilled through drinking hemlock.

[57] Plato (427–347BC). Wealthy Athenian philosopher who began as a student of Socrates. After the death of his master, he studied abroad with the students of Pythagoras until he set up his own school of philosophy in Athens. Although he regarded himself as a socratic thinker, he developed his mentor's thought significantly, though with substantial faithfulness to it, such that he and his disciples are referred to as "major socratics." His chief contribution to Philosophy was to develop it into a complete and coherent system, even if not one free from errors. His wisdom and intuition ensured that the errors that were to be found in his system did not obscure the essential truth that it contained, such that great thinkers like St. Augustine were able (as Maritain says) "to extract from Plato's gold-mine the ore of truth." Important works include *Timaeus*, *The Laws*, and *The Republic*.

[58] Marcus Aurelius Antoninus (121–180). Became a Roman Consul in 140, before becoming Emperor (161). A man of noble character, a committed adherent of Stoic philosophy, and one interested more in study than in governance. His elevation to the throne marked the end of the *Pax Romana* which had been so happy and fruitful

under the Antonines. Problems of all kinds invaded the Empire in Britain and the Orient, and from beyond the Rhine and the Danube. His son was the unworthy wretch, Commodus, who became Emperor in his turn.

[59] Constantine the Great (274?–337). Flavius Valerius Constantinus became Roman Emperor in 306, and immediately had to combat a number of rival claimants within the Empire. In his clash with Maxentius at Milvian Bridge in 312, he ordered that the shields of his mostly pagan troops should be inscribed with the monogram of Christ (X P from the word *Christos*) because of a vision he received which declared, "In this sign wilt thou conquer." The Edict of Milan (313) demonstrated his gratitude; it declared the toleration of Christians within the Empire. By 325 he had defeated the other claimants to the throne, and he set about works of construction. He began the building of Constantinople (modern-day Istanbul) which was to be the centre of the Empire, and devoted himself to the moral, political, and economic welfare of his subjects. Interested in art and literature, he greatly assisted the development of Catholicism, although he was only baptised in the year of his death.

[60] Joseph McCabe (1867–1955). English Franciscan who left the priesthood in great anger in 1896, thereafter becoming a virulent and venomous critic of the Church. A founding member of the British Rationalist Press and a prolific writer and speaker who (it is believed) gave over 3,000 lectures during his lifetime. His Atheism strengthened over his lifetime and is reflected in his more than 30 books.

[61] Albigensianism (also known as Catharism). A heresy which appeared in 12th-century Provence, in the South of France. It was a Manichean doctrine positing God against the Evil One, Light against Dark, and the Soul against the Body, all in *unending* conflict, based ultimately upon the premise that preached that matter is evil and spirit is good. Given that food, sex, etc. – as material things – were "evil," the highest object in life was to escape from the Body. The most ascetic Albigensians, called the Perfects, sought death through ritual starvation. Both St. Dominic and St. Bernard were sent to the region to preach to the heretics. In 1208, Pope Innocent III declared a crusade against the Cathars and Raymond VI of Toulouse, their principal civil supporter. Within a century the heresy had been completely uprooted, though the crusade itself, despite Innocent III's best efforts, was not free from regrettable excesses and at times it degenerated into a mere war of conquest. In the process, the Inquisition had come into being (1229) and passed into Dominican hands, by which means they were to look after the final suppression of the heresy.

[62] Pope Innocent III (1160–1216). One of the greatest of the medieval Popes. Born Lotario de'Conti, the son of Count Trasimund of Segni in Italy, he was renowned for his deep piety and for his great knowledge of men. He became Pope, with great reluctance, in 1198. At that time the Imperial Throne was vacant due to the death of Henry VI in 1197, so Innocent moved quickly to re-establish papal power both in Rome and within the Papal States. Thereafter he was continually active in the affairs of countries far and wide: Spain, Poland, Hungary, Sweden, and the Germanies. During his reign he sanctioned the founding of the Dominican and Franciscan Orders; he founded the Santo Spirito hospital in Sassia in Italy – which still exists – and which was a model for future city hospitals; he convoked the Fourth Lateran Council which condemned the Albigensian and Waldensian heresies; he gave the first official ecclesiastical sanction to the word "transubstantiation"; and he launched the Fourth Crusade to free the Holy Land.

About IHS Press

IHS Press believes that the key to the restoration of Catholic Society is the recovery and the implementation of the wisdom our Fathers in the Faith possessed so fully less than a century ago. At a time when numerous ideologies were competing for supremacy, these men articulated, with precision and vigor, and *without* apology or compromise, the only genuine alternative to the then- (and still-) prevailing currents of thought: value-free and yet bureaucratic "progressivism" on the one hand, and the rehashed, *laissez-faire* free-for-all of "conservatism" on the other. That alternative is the Social Teaching of the Catholic Church.

Catholic Social Teaching offers the solutions to the political, economic, and social problems that plague modern society; problems that stem from the false principles of the Reformation, Renaissance, and Revolution, and which are exacerbated by the industrialization and the secularization of society that has continued for several centuries. Defending, explaining, and applying this Teaching was the business of the great Social Catholics of last century. Unfortunately, much of their work is today both unknown and unavailable.

Thus, IHS Press was founded in September of 2001A.D. as the only publisher dedicated exclusively to the Social Teaching of the Church, helping Catholics of the third millennium pick up where those of last century left off. IHS Press is committed to recovering, and *helping others to rediscover,* the valuable works of the Catholic economists, historians, and social critics. To that end, IHS Press is in the business of issuing critical editions of works on society, politics, and economics by writers, thinkers, and men of action such as Hilaire Belloc, Gilbert Chesterton, Arthur Penty, Fr. Vincent McNabb, Fr. Denis Fahey, Jean Ousset, Amintore Fanfani, George O'Brien, and others, making the wisdom they contain available to the current generation.

It is the aim of IHS Press to issue these vitally important works in high-quality volumes and at reasonable prices, to enable the widest possible audience to acquire, enjoy, and benefit from them. Such an undertaking cannot be maintained without the support of generous benefactors. With that in mind, IHS Press was constituted as a not-for-profit corporation which is exempt from federal tax according to Section 501(c)(3) of the United States Internal Revenue Code. Donations to IHS Press are, therefore, tax deductible, and are especially welcome to support its continued operation, and to help it with the publication of new titles and the more widespread dissemination of those already in print.

For more information, contact us at:

222 W. 21ˢᵗ St., Suite F-122~Norfolk, VA 23517~(757) 423-0324
info@ihspress.com   www.ihspress.com   fax: (800) 364-0186

IHS Press is a tax-exempt 501(c)(3) corporation; EIN: 54-2057581.
Applicable documentation is available upon request.